PACIFIC OCEAN

0   50   100
Miles

GE
99
KLAMATH
MOUNTAINS

TRINITY
NATIONAL
FOREST
TRINITY
ALPS
WILDERNESS
MARBLE MOUNTAIN
WILDERNESS
Seiad Valley

299

Castle Crags
State Park

SHASTA
NATIONAL
FOREST
Mount
Shasta
(14,162 ft.)

Ashland

Mount McLoughlin
(9,495 ft.)

299

SHASTA
NATIONAL
FOREST

97

Burney Falls
State Park

CRATER LAKE
NATIONAL PARK

138

58

SKY LAKES
WILDERNESS

140

CRATER
LAKE

Diamond
Lake Lodge

126

20

THREE
SISTERS
WILDERNESS

North Sister
(10,085 ft.)

EUGENE

WILLAMETTE RIVER

101

26

PORTLAND

Mount Thielsen
(9,182 ft.)

Willamette Pass (5,126 ft.)

South Sister (10,358 ft.)

Elk Lake
Resort

Middle
Sister
(10,047 ft.)

Yapoah
Crater

Collier Cone

Three Fingered Jack
(7,841 ft.)

Jude
Lake

Mt.
Jefferson
(10,497 ft.)

Timberline
Lodge

Cascade
Locks

R

INDIAN
HEAVEN
WILDERNESS

12

Mt. St. Helens
(8,364 ft.)

12

5

101

SEATTLE

410

MT.
RAINIER
NATIONAL
PARK

G

140

91

BEND

26

20

97

84

Mt.
Hood
(11,235 ft.)

Mt.
Adams
(12,276 ft.)

GOAT ROCKS
WILDERNESS

Mt. Rainier
(14,410 ft.)

Chinook Pass (5,432 ft.)

Tieton
Pass
(4,570 ft.)

White
Pass
(4,500 ft.)

410

90

2

20

Snoqualmie Pass (3,127 ft.)

Skykomish

ALPINE LAKES
WILDERNESS

Stevens
Pass
(4,061 ft.)

Glacier
Pk.
(10,544 ft.)

Red Pass
(6,500 ft.)

N CASCADE
MOUNTAINS

Ross Lake

Rainy Pass (4,860 ft.)

Stehekin

Mazama

Manning
Park

1

82

12

LAKE
CHELAN

OREGON

CHAPTER 4

395

20

97

90

WASHINGTON

CHAPTER 5

I D A H O

BOISE

95

84

SPOKANE

90

VANCOUVER ISLAND

VICTORIA

VANCOUVER

101

C A N A D A

3

97

D0744155

Along the *Pacific Crest Trail*

PHOTOGRAPHY BY BART SMITH

TEXT BY KAREN BERGER AND DANIEL R. SMITH

FOREWORD BY BOB BALLOU

EXECUTIVE DIRECTOR OF THE PACIFIC CREST TRAIL ASSOCIATION

CONTENTS

WESTCLIFFE PUBLISHERS

ENGLEWOOD, COLORADO

ISBN: 1-56579-277-7

Designers: Tim George and Mark Mulvany
Map Designer: John Wagner
Production Manager: Harlene Finn
Editor: Kiki Sayre

Published by: Westcliffe Publishers, Inc.
P.O. Box 1261
Englewood, Colorado 80150

Printed in Hong Kong by Palace Press International

Library of Congress Cataloging-in-Publication Data

Smith, Bart, 1959–
      Along the Pacific Crest Trail / photography by Bart Smith ; text
by Karen Berger and Daniel R. Smith ; foreword by Bob Ballou.
          p. cm.
      ISBN 1-56579-277-7
      1. Smith, Bart, 1959– —Journeys—Pacific Crest Trail—
Guidebooks. 2. Berger, Karen, 1959– —Journeys—Pacific Crest
Trail—Guidebooks. 3. Hiking—Pacific Crest Trail—Guidebooks.
4. Pacific Crest Trail—Description and travel. 5. Pacific Crest
Trail—Guidebooks. I. Berger, Karen, 1959– . II. Smith, Daniel
R. (Daniel Richard) III. Title.
GV199.42.P3S65 1998
917.9—dc21
                                                                            98-9590
                                                                               CIP

For more information about other fine books and calendars from Westcliffe Publishers, please call your local bookstore, contact us at 1-800-523-3692, or write for our free color catalog.

First frontis: *Looking north from Mount Laguna, Laguna Mountains, California*

Second frontis: *California poppies near Warner Springs, California*

Page 3:   *On the Trail just outside Indian Heaven Wilderness, Washington*

Opposite: *Bighorn Plateau, Sequoia National Park, California*

ACKNOWLEDGMENTS

We hikers like to think of ourselves as tough individualists, who walk away from the everyday world into the freedom of the mountains. But without a whole lot of help from a whole lot of people, we would not have been able to undertake our journey, let alone this book. We owe a huge debt of gratitude.

Thank you to Pat Lisella, for yet again managing our food drops and gear resupplies, and to Linda Soldatos, for managing the home front; to Anne and Steve Emry, who coped with our long list of requests to receive this package or mail that one; to Jeff "Trapper" Robbins (mountain golfer extraordinaire) and Roxanne Everett, for handling yet more boxes, and for hosting us while we were in Seattle; to Cameron Billecci, for shipping us gear, lending us equipment, responding to our pleas for help, and showing up on the trail with a pickup truck full of food— also for letting us rifle through his library and borrow books for our research; to Mike Halloran, Brian Nickerson, and Brian Siesto, for research and library help; to Peg Spry in Agua Dulce, for driving Karen all over southern California to find medical help for her foot; and also in Agua Dulce, to Joan Byrd and Bernice Canutt at the Century 21, for being friends to hikers; to Bob Ballou and Joe Sobinovksy at the PCTA, who answered our requests for information; to Larry Cash and Louise Marshall, for sharing their memories of the early days of the PCT; to everyone who volunteers to maintain the trail, for making our journey possible in the first place; to Bart Smith, who conceived the idea for this book, for his fine hospitality and help at the end of our trip; to Iona College, for support through its Faculty Fellowship Program; and also at Iona, to the professionals in the Computer Services Center and at Ryan Library, for assistance and advice; to Al and Alison Alsdorf, for letting us use their computer and printer; to Judie and John Efono, for their hospitality; and to the fine staff at Westcliffe, especially Kiki Sayre and Linda Doyle, for their flexibility and professionalism.

Finally, a huge thank you to our wonderful friends, Bob and Dorlyn Williams, who invited us to be artists in residence in their home when we needed a place to write.

—KAREN BERGER AND DANIEL R. SMITH

This book is dedicated to Pat Lisella and Linda Soldatos, for help beyond the call of friendship.

Lower Palisades Lake, Kings Canyon National Park, California

FOREWORD

"Pacific Crest National Scenic Trail"—the words evoke an image of a special trail with vistas of azure-blue lakes, lush alpine meadows, and snowcapped peaks. Surely, that was Clinton Clarke's vision when he organized the Pacific Crest Trail System Conference in 1932.

Bart Smith has captured that vision on film. Karen Berger and Dan Smith have put into words the thrill and the agony of a long walk through remote and desolate places. As we leaf through this magnificent book, we owe a debt of gratitude not just to the photographer, authors, and publisher, but to Clarke and those who followed him. We should reflect for a moment on the making and keeping of this trail.

What began as an effort to link several planned or then existent trails—Cascade Crest, Oregon Skyline, Lava Crest, Tahoe-Yosemite, John Muir, Sierra, and Desert Crest—continues today as the Pacific Crest Trail Association strives to preserve and protect the trail from urban encroachment and land management practices that debase the users' experience.

Clarke's conference lobbied the federal government to create a ten-mile-wide corridor for the trail, but the cost was too great. Vision and reality clashed. Reality won. Clarke and the conference died in 1957, but the vision of a border-to-border trail lived on.

In February 1965, President Lyndon Johnson called for the development and protection of a balanced system of trails to help protect and enhance the total quality of the outdoor environment, as well as to provide much needed opportunities for healthful outdoor recreation.

A task force representing four agencies with jurisdiction over federal lands was appointed to conduct a study, and in December 1966 the results were published as "Trails for America." In its recommendations, the task force said:

Each [national scenic trail] should stand out in its own right as a recreation resource . . . be built to harmonize with the natural areas they cross . . . and afford the visitor closeup instruction in nature and her ways. The entire length of each, together with sufficient land area on both sides to safeguard adequately and preserve its character, should be protected in some form of public control. Federal and state agencies should modify timber harvesting, livestock grazing, and special permit practices to protect trail quality . . . and the natural and scenic qualities and historic features along and near national scenic trails must be protected.

"Trails for America" provided the basic language for what was to become the National Trails System Act, but testimony during congressional hearings resulted in a reversal of priorities. The Act passed by Congress on 2 October 1968 states, "In selecting rights-of-way, full consideration shall be given to minimizing the [trail's] adverse effects upon the adjacent landowner or user and his operation. Development and management of each segment of the National Trails System shall be designed to harmonize with and complement any established multiple-use plans for the specific area in order to ensure continued maximum benefits from the land."

An Advisory Council was appointed to work with federal agencies. A new Pacific Crest Trail Conference was organized by Clarke's protégé, Warren Rogers, to advise hikers and equestrians on use of the trail. Members helped with construction, and the trail, though not entirely protected on federal land, was finally completed in 1993. The conference became the association, bringing together visionaries and a new generation of outdoor enthusiasts who were concerned with protecting this national treasure. A formal mission statement was adopted to guide them in their efforts:

The mission of the Pacific Crest Trail Association is to promote and protect the Pacific Crest National Scenic Trail so as to reflect its world-class significance for the enjoyment, education and adventure of hikers and equestrians.

A Memorandum of Understanding, recognizing the association as the "government's major partner in the operation of the trail," was signed with the Forest Service, National Park Service, and Bureau of Land Management.

The Pacific Crest Trail Association has made significant strides in attracting and involving trail enthusiasts in this mission. Utilizing volunteer resources and modern technology, it created an Internet website that offers up-to-date information on trail conditions and links to other sites with information for hikers and equestrians: www.gorp.com/pcta. For those without Internet access, a toll-free telephone hotline provides trail condition reports 24-hours-a-day: (888)PCTRAIL.

Volunteer trail crews dedicate thousands of hours each year to clearing and repairing the trail. Most importantly, the association is addressing the ongoing issues of timber harvesting and urban encroachment on public and privately held sections of the trail. This work is made possible by a dedicated board of directors, the financial support of its donors, the diligence of its members, and you—because a portion of the proceeds from the sale of this book will benefit the Pacific Crest Trail Association.

Now, enjoy your journey on the Pacific Crest National Scenic Trail.

—ROBERT BALLOU

Moss-covered Spruce, Three Sisters Wilderness, Oregon

PREFACE

I first became aware of the Pacific Crest Trail when I was 13 years old. I was hiking with my Scout troop on our annual 50-miler in the Cascade Mountains when we crossed a north/south trail just north of Snoqualmie Pass. I wouldn't have given much thought to it, except that our Scout master mentioned if we were to follow this trail to its southern end we would be at the Mexican border. The trail was called the Pacific Crest Trail. In our amazement, my eyes followed the trail to the southern horizon.

Through the years I often crossed paths with the Pacific Crest Trail and I would always think of the country awaiting. Places like Mount St. Helens, the Columbia River Gorge, Mount Jefferson, Mount Shasta, Yosemite, Mount Whitney and the Mojave Desert all beckoned to me to follow that trail.

Twenty years after that first encounter, I began planning my Pacific Crest trek. From the outset I foresaw the journey as a combination of two of my lifelong passions: hiking and photography. I wanted to experience the satisfaction of seeing Mount Rainier growing from a speck on the horizon, to its massive size with its glaciers looming over me, and then to a speck on the horizon behind me, and know that I walked all those miles. I wanted to experience the thrill of capturing on film as much of the infinite and fleeting beauty along the Pacific Crest Trail as I could.

What I didn't foresee was that my one-year trek would turn into a six-year mission. Shortly into my first month of hiking the trail, it became apparent that long-distance hiking and wilderness photography are in many ways incompatible. Long-distance hiking requires adhering to a set schedule and a heavy pack. Wilderness photography requires spontaneity, patience, and a heavier pack. After viewing the photographs from my first year, I decided to finish hiking the trail the following year and then take as many years as necessary to rehike the trail in short sections allowing time to properly photograph the environs in their best light and seasonal display. In short, photographing along the Pacific Crest Trail with my tripod, Nikon F3, and five lenses would become a labor of love.

I have grown very fond of this 2658-mile ribbon called the Pacific Crest Trail. Like so many things in life, the trail can demand a tremendous amount of effort and discomfort, but sometimes it's that very sacrifice that makes the rewards so much sweeter. I've hobbled down the trail, run down the trail, cursed the trail, and kissed the trail—and always felt alive and fortunate to witness the awesome land, sky, and life that the Pacific Crest Trail touches. It's my hope that the images in this book will provide evidence of the visual feast awaiting those who spend a day, a weekend, or six months walking the Pacific Crest Trail.

When I heard that Karen Berger and Dan Smith were hiking the trail and would contribute the story of their journey to this book, I became a strong believer in serendipity. I had long been looking for someone who could appropriately convey the trials and rewards of hiking the Pacific Crest Trail in six months. Successful writers of backpacking experiences are a select group, and to have Karen Berger, one of the genre's eminent writers, contributing to this book is more than I could have wished for. Dan brings the added dimension of historical, geological and geographical insight, which enriches the narrative with a strong sense of place along the trail.

The photographs and narrative follow the Pacific Crest Trail chronologically starting near Campo at the Mexican border and heading north to Manning Park, Canada. Photographs taken by Dan provide the visual support for Karen and Dan's journey, while my images are chronologically supportive but independent of the narrative. The majority of my photographs were taken either on or within one-quarter mile of the Pacific Crest Trail; however, I did take the liberty to photograph scenic side trips, as well. The furthest I ventured from the trail was 4 miles.

When I told my wife Bridgie about my idea of photographing the Pacific Crest Trail for a possible book, she didn't laugh (out loud), but rather purchased a new backpack, boots, and a food dehydrator to help support my project. Bridgie would eventually cook and dehydrate hundreds of meals, and all except two were delicious (cod and peppered cream corn were not meant to be dehydrated). She mailed food drops to post offices on or near the trail and, more importantly, took care of the home front all those months I was on the trail. Without her help this project would not have been possible.

I would also like to thank Lou and Betty Reccow, for their companionship from the Tehachapi through Kennedy Meadows—it was heartening to see other crazed humans attempting that section in July; Ray Pfortner from Art Wolf, Inc., for giving me a big boost in confidence regarding the validity of my project and photography; and my employers, Bob Losinger and Craig Milton, for holding my job all the months I was away. Finally, I would be remiss if I didn't thank the countless people who worked building the Pacific Crest Trail and the volunteers who maintain it today. The Pacific Crest Trail Association recruits volunteers for trail maintenance; it is an awesome task maintaining 2,658 miles of trail, and they can always use more volunteers. The rewards are companionship, beautiful country and the satisfaction that comes with hard work. A big thank you to all the volunteers at the PCTA.

I would like to dedicate my contribution to this book to my wife Bridgie Graham-Smith, whose support was indispensable, and to the memory of my father David W. Smith, who taught me photography with his love of the outdoors and his Kine Exacta camera.

—BART SMITH

Pasque flowers and Mount Rainier, Mount Rainier National Park, Washington

INTRODUCTION

Big dreams: everybody has them. Sailing around the world; singing in a rock concert; learning to speak French; living in a house in Tuscany—or walking from Mexico to Canada on the Pacific Crest Trail: 2,658 miles through the great mountain ranges of California, Oregon, and Washington.

That was our dream in the spring of 1997.

You might call us backpacking junkies. Dan had hiked the PCT in three long sections during the summers of 1984-1986; he had also previously hiked the Appalachian Trail (five times) and the Continental Divide. For Dan, this was the chance to thru-hike the PCT all in one journey.

For Karen, it was the chance to complete backpacking's triple crown—hikes of the Appalachian, Pacific Crest, and Continental Divide National Scenic Trails.

But the real motivation for a thru-hike has to go deeper than that. There's no way you're going to walk 2,600 miles through deserts, snowfields, heat waves, cold snaps, and a month of rain just for bragging rights.

The simple truth is that we love to live in the woods. For 10 years, we have been stealing away to the wilderness together, for days or weekends, and sometimes for weeks or months. Hiking has become a way of life. Especially, we love long walks, where time slows to a crawl, and the universe is inexorably whittled away until all that remains is the current moment: the views, the wind, the birdsong, the feeling of muscles working and resting, the blackness of the sky, and the brightness of the moon. We know of no better way to live in the present than to walk in the mountains.

Supreme Court Justice William O. Douglas, an avid hiker, once wrote:

> *The thrill of tramping alone and unafraid through a wilderness of lakes, creeks, alpine meadows, and glaciers is not known to many. A civilization can be built around the machine but it is doubtful that a meaningful life can be produced by it . . . When man worships at the feet of avalanche lilies or discovers the delicacies of the pasque flower or finds the faint perfume of the phlox on rocky ridges, he will come to know that the real glories are God's creations. When he feels the wind blowing through him on a high peak or sleeps under a closely matted white bark pine in an exposed basin, he is apt to find his relationship to the universe.*

The National Scenic Trails System helps us to do that.

Passed by Congress in 1968, the National Trails System Act named the Appalachian Trail and the Pacific Crest Trail as the first two national scenic trails. Today, there are eight of these long distance footways, most of them still in various stages of route selection and construction. The AT and the PCT are the only ones that can lay claim to a complete route.

It's taken a long time to be able to make that claim. The genesis of the PCT can be traced back to 1915, a year after the death of conservationist John Muir, when the California legislature approved funds for a trail to follow the main crest of the High Sierra. The John Muir Trail, completed in 1934, runs from Mount Whitney to Yosemite Valley, and was one of the PCT's earliest links. In 1920, work began on the Oregon Skyline Trail, which would ultimately run the entire length of Oregon; in 1928, Washington followed, with its border-to-border Cascade Crest Trail.

In the late 1920s, perhaps inspired by the efforts underway in the East to construct the Appalachian Trail, members of western hiking clubs started talking about a trail to follow the mountain backbones of California, Oregon, and Washington. In 1932, trail enthusiast Clinton Clarke proposed the idea to the national park and forest services, and the project was underway. Three years later, Clarke created the Pacific Crest Trailway System Conference, which he headed until his death in 1957. One of Clarke's earliest projects, from 1935 to 1938, was a series of relays, or tag teams, in which groups of YMCA members scouted a route for the trail—and in the process covered the entire distance from Mexico to Canada. In 1945, Clarke published a handbook based on the relays, but it gave only general directions, not details. It did, however, articulate a rationale for the trail that has not changed in the intervening half century:

> *In few places in the world—certainly nowhere else in the United States —are found such a varied and priceless collection of sculptured master-pieces of Nature as adorn, strung like pearls, the mountain ranges of Washington, Oregon, and California. The Pacific Crest Trailway is the cord that binds the necklace, each gem encased in a permanent wilderness protected from all mechanization and commercialization.*

After Clarke's death, the torch passed to Warren Rogers, one of Clarke's associates in the relay project. Like Clarke, Rogers remained a lifelong PCT activist and organizer. For the first few years, however, work progressed slowly, especially in California. New life was breathed into the old project in 1965, when the Bureau of Outdoor Recreation proposed a national system of trails, and in 1968, with the passage of the National Trails System Act.

Finally, in the early 1970s, a combination of factors coalesced to bring the trail to public attention and, ultimately, completion. A Citizen's Advisory Council was appointed to manage route selection. Nationwide, a growing interest in backpacking brought more people to the trail. The Pacific Crest Trail Club was formed for hikers. And the first thru-hikers made the border-to-border pilgrimage from Mexico to Canada.

In 1977, Rogers founded the Pacific Crest Trail Association, which is responsible for managing the trail in cooperation with the U.S. Forest Service. In the 1970s, 1980s, and early 1990s, its focus was the mammoth job of actually building the miles and miles of trail. Finally, in 1993, a Golden Spike Ceremony in southern California's Soledad Canyon celebrated the completion of the trail.

Today, the Pacific Crest Trail runs through 24 national forests, seven national parks, a national recreation area, a national monument, 33 wildernesses, six state and provincial parks, four BLM management areas, and dozens of parcels of private land. It passes through desert valleys, over cloud-piercing granite mountains, through volcanic lava fields, into misty, ancient Cascadian forests that hold up the sky. To hike it will make you tired, hungry, thirsty, hot, cold, wet, strong, exhilarated, surprised, awe-struck, humble, and proud.

Come with us, and enjoy the trip.

—KAREN BERGER AND DANIEL R. SMITH

On the Trail looking south, Cottonwood Valley

chapter 1

SOUTHERN CALIFORNIA: DRYLANDS

"You sure this is it?"

The taxi driver looks at us as though there's something unusual about our destination.

Dan, who has been here before, is studying the guidebook and the landscape. Suddenly, he spots a clearing.

"Stop! I remember this pile of tires."

"That particular pile of tires?" I ask. Dan was last here nine years ago. Then again, this sagebrush scrubland looks like the kind of place where a pile of tires might just sit around undisturbed for a decade or three.

We jump out of the cab while the driver shakes his head.

"Glad it's you and not me," he says.

A few yards south of the clearing, two parallel barbed-wire fences slice through the landscape. They mark the border—on this side the United States, on that side Mexico. I half expect the two sides to look different, like in those maps from elementary school where each country is a clearly delineated block of color. Here, color is a rare thing. On both sides of the border, khaki-hued chaparral and dry, dun earth stretch to the far horizons; if you want more color than that, you have to look up, to the sky, or settle for the greener grasses of metaphor.

My attention shifts from the fence to a modest wooden monument a few feet away. Its text confirms our location: "Pacific Crest Trail: Mexico to Canada."

And written in our data book, some numbers that refuse to fit into my brain. 2,658.

That's 2,658 miles.

Which we intend to walk.

A small notebook is tucked into a cubby-hole carved into the monument. It's a trail register. Over the next few months, these communal diaries will serve as a forum for debate, a source of humor, an outlet for complaints, and the trellis of the hiker grapevine. Some 60 people have signed in ahead of us. For the most part, the words are banal.

"Headed to Canada, sure hope I make it."

"Wow, can't believe I'm finally here."

When I start to add my message, I understand the problem: the act of committing the journey to paper, of standing here in the middle of dusty nowhere and declaring that we intend to walk each one of those 2,658 miles, is abruptly overwhelming. An acute case of writer's block prevents me from offering something profound and unique. I have to settle for signing my name and sending my best wishes to our fellow hikers. Dan adds his name under mine, as lost for words as I am.

Two thousand six hundred and fifty-eight miles. Six million steps, more or less. I feel a strange reluctance to take the first one, so I find reasons to dally. I stick one foot through the strands of the barbed wire fence to touch Mexican soil. Dan takes pictures: of me, of the monument, of the two of us together, of the fence. I glance at the little thermometer that hangs from a zipper-pull on my pack. Ninety degrees. It's only 10 o'clock in the morning.

Enough dithering.

"Ready?" Dan asks.

I take a long look south into Mexico, then turn my back on the fence.

"Ready or not," I say.

We heft our packs. Mine lands on my back with the force of a thousand regrets.

"Oh, Lord," I think, "I'm in trouble now."

Trail lore has it that the only way to get ready to backpack up a mountain is to put on a pack and walk up a mountain. This is about as sensible as saying the only way to get ready to run a marathon is to run a marathon, but as with so many myths, there is a kernel of truth at the core: Short of being a full-time athlete, no exercise program can really prepare you to walk 2,600 miles.

Take, as exhibit A, the first day. The distance between the border and the next guaranteed source of water is 20 miles, including 3,000 feet of elevation gain. (Figure most of a marathon including two and a half trips up and down the Empire State Building in 90-degree heat with a pack on your back.) You can either knock off the entire distance in one day or carry enough water for however long it's going to take you to get there. Neither choice makes for easy walking if your prick fitness program has been composed mostly of good intentions.

I should have known better—did, in fact, know better. This isn't my first long-distance hike, and it's not the first time I've showed up at the trailhead looking like the "before" picture in a diet commercial. I know all about the rebellion that soft and citified muscles can mount when confronted with the physical demands of backpacking. I know this from personal, painful experience—experience from which I have somehow managed to learn exactly nothing. Now, the weight on my back is sending me a clear and ominous message: It's payback time.

Dan, who runs 70 miles a week, including 20 every Saturday, very kindly avoids saying I told you so.

Fitness notwithstanding, the packs are heavy. Over the last few months, Dan and I have had endless discussions: tarps versus tents, hiking shoes versus boots, which kind of stove, water filter, sleeping bag, camping mattress . . . Our key requirement is flexibility. In the drylands of southern California, the Pacific Crest Trail undulates between 1,200 and 9,000 feet in elevation. Since every thousand feet of elevation gain is more or less equal—in ecological terms—to going 170 miles north, the trail passes through a variety of ecosystems, from a lower Sonora environment filled with cactus and creosote to sylvan ridges not dissimilar to the forests of northern Canada. Sometimes, we'll walk from one to the other in a single day.

And that's just in the first 650 miles. Farther north, in the dizzying heights of the still snow-bound Sierra Nevada, the Pacific Crest Trail ascends to sky-scraping elevations: 11,000, 12,000, and 13,000 feet above sea level. To negotiate the high passes, we'll need ice axes; to cross swollen snowmelt-fed streams, we'll use trekking sticks and a prayer. We'll also need warmer clothes for the cold mountain nights and a tent to protect us from hordes of snowmelt-bred mosquitoes.

Summer will find us in the high country of northern California and Oregon, where our major concern will be making hay—or, in this case, mileage—while the sun shines. Sending home extra gear to lighten our loads, we'll try to make it to the lush Cascadian forests of Washington before they are drenched by autumn rains. Or covered with snow. Winter storms can begin as early as September; the toponyms—Frosty Pass, Foggy Pass, Windy Pass, Rainy Pass, Blizzard Peak, Freezeout Mountain, and Early Winters Pass—tell us everything we need to know.

Heading north along the Trail, Laguna Mountains

View of Anza-Borrego Desert from Garnet Peak, Laguna Mountains

Barrel cactus display, Anza-Borrego Desert State Park

Throughout the months ahead, we'll adjust our gear as the conditions change. To start, we've settled on a tarp rather than a tent, because we're more concerned about protection from the midday sun than from rain or insects. For night, we have summer-weight sleeping bags, whose temperature ratings can be bolstered with a couple of extra layers of clothing. Doing double duty for bug and sun protection are light-colored, light-weight synthetic pants and long-sleeved shirts, which we've dubbed our shade suits. We're also carrying rain gear because soggy experience has taught us that we never want to be without it.

Next, there's the bare-bones collection that passes for our kitchen: one 2-quart pot with lid, a couple of plastic bowls, two spoons, one potholder, and a scouring pad. Our multi-fuel camp stove can run on white gas, kerosene, or even unleaded gas from a service station. Finally, a water filter ensures that we can drink from virtually any water source we encounter, no matter how polluted—that is, until the filter clogs, sputters, leaks, or otherwise rebels against the inevitable accumulation of cow dung, pond scum, algae, and grime, not to mention microscopic cooties like *Giardia, Cryptosporidium,* and whatever that bacteria is that turns alpine snow watermelon pink.

This basic gear, including packs, maps, camera, ground cloth, and various miscellany, plus food and water, weighs about 40 pounds for each of us (although the way we actually divide it up, Dan carries more—his reward for being in better shape than I am). No matter how many times we sift through the equipment, there's not a single item we consider extraneous. Food weight is about 2 pounds per person a day—in this case, 8 pounds each. But the real loadhog, at 2 pounds per quart, is water.

If you've done most of your hiking in temperate forests and mountains, which is where most sane people do most of their hiking, you're probably not in the habit of keeping track of your water supply as though you were watching the fuel gauge in a rusty old gas guzzler that has to cross a 300-mile desert on a 10-gallon tank. You're probably used to drinking when you're thirsty, filling up when your bottle is empty, and assuming that if there's a dry stretch ahead, your guidebook will give you plenty of advance notice.

Here in southern California, the entire trail is a dry stretch. The distance between one water source and the next can be 20 miles; 25 or 30 is not unheard of. And that mileage might include a climb of 5,000 feet just to make things interesting.

After the border, the first reliable water source is Lake Morena County Park, 20 miles away. We expect to arrive there midday tomorrow. That means we need enough water for walking, dinner, breakfast, and sleeping. Park rangers typically recommend 8 quarts of water per day for hot-weather desert hiking. The only trouble with that piece of advice is what it adds up to: 16 pounds per person. Per day.

Our total water-carrying capacity is 15 quarts: one 8-quart fabric sack, two 2-quart sacks, and three 1-quart Nalgene bottles. Based on our previous desert hiking experience, which has been considerable, we decide to drink as much as we can—about 3 quarts each—in the cab, and carry 5 quarts each—about 10 pounds. That's a little skimpy, but this early in the season, there's a chance we'll encounter water in one of the seasonal creeks along the way. If we do, we can swill to our heart's content. If we don't, we'll need to ration our supply.

All of which sounds like a good plan when we're guzzling water in the taxi. But once the driver has waved good-bye and we've actually started walking—once we have struck out into the dusty dry lands with exactly the amount of water that is sloshing on our backs and in our stomachs and not one drop more—nagging little water-logged questions start seeping around the edges of my brain. Should we have taken another couple of quarts? Is it only my imagination, or has the temperature actually risen in the last half hour? Should I have paid closer attention to the elevation gains? Why does the back of my throat feel like it's suddenly coated with cobwebs?

When the cobwebs have taken over my entire mouth, I stop to drink and manage to gulp down a whole quart in a matter of seconds. So much for rationing. That's 2 pounds off my back, but it's also one-fifth of my water supply. We've been walking exactly an hour and a half.

Fortunately, nature is in a generous mood: a few minutes later, after our water break, we cross a gully of damp dirt that passes for a stream a few months each year. The creekbed is surrounded by a jungle of cattails and willows, so green it looks positively Amazonian. Under the shade of a cottonwood tree we find a small pool of water that has not yet finished evaporating.

My shirt is soaked with sweat and I am breathing hard from the exertion. Within seconds, I swill another quart. I had hoped that my lack of fitness would go unnoticed if I simply pushed

Agave and barrel cactus, Anza-Borrego Desert State Park

Along the Trail near Warner Springs, San Jose Del Valle

through the first few days of aches and pains without complaining, but my gasping lungs betray me. So does my face. Dan notes that it is the approximate color of a ripe cherry.

"I'm okay," I tell him.

Once again, he avoids saying I told you so.

Our plan for this first day is to dry camp about 11 miles from the border. So far, we've walked about 3 miles, but there's no rush. We could sit in this delicious pool of shade all afternoon, hiding from the sun, and we'd still have plenty of time to walk those last 8 miles in the cooler evening hours. No matter. Over the course of 10 years as hiking partners, Dan and I have developed one or two fairly inviolable habits, and one of them is that we don't stop for lunch after hiking a measly 3 miles. We walk on.

The landscape, of course, is indifferent to our habits.

"Fine," it seems to say. "Go ahead. Walk past a shady, watered lunch spot in the middle of the day. But don't expect to find another one."

Indeed, there are no other shady spots. No other trees. Not even a cloud to give occasional relief as the sun blazes across the sky. There is just the endless carpet of waist-high chaparral, which offers the kind of shade you'd get if you sat under a lace curtain. Adjectives from the guidebook float through my brain: mind-broiling, furnace-breathed, scorching, blistering. I'm not feeling any need to quibble with the authors' choice of words.

I am trying to not think about what it will mean to walk through 650 miles of this, day after day after day—and then 2,000 more miles after that. I am trying to tell myself that this is the break-in period, that breaking in is always tough; and besides, what did I expect, coming out here to walk across the country when I can barely jog around the block?

Through all of my long hikes, I have always wondered about people who start a long trail and—having done all the planning, having packed their supplies, bought their gear, quit their jobs, sublet their apartments, rented out their houses, sold their cars—quit after a mere few days. This is as close to understanding as I have ever come. In the back of my mind, a small voice is saying: "I don't have to do this. I can go somewhere else. Like Tahiti."

But there are certain things I know. I know that in a few days my body will adjust to the heat. My feet will get used to the boots and my back to my pack, and my muscles will remember how to pace themselves so that I can climb a mountain without gasping for breath. I will relearn the lessons of the landscape: to drink when there is water, to rest when there is shade, to walk in the cooler hours of morning and evening. The effort of walking will fade into the background, becoming a constant accompaniment to the hike, but no longer its melody. Issues I now wrestle with—pack weight and water and boot fit and where everything goes in the pack—will slide into well-worn routines, leaving me free to pursue the simple goals of long-distance hiking. Benton MacKaye, founder of the Appalachian Trail, said them best: "To walk, to see, and to see what you see."

May 6. Day 1. Mile 11.5. Northeast ridge of Hauser Mountain.

It seems like I left New York a year ago, so completely has the desert erased the memory of prick hustle and last-minute urgencies. Now, a pressing decision means choosing whether to use water when we brush our teeth. An emergency is treating a hot spot that might decide to become a blister. Our life is boiled down to essentials: food, water, shelter from the sun. A week ago, we sat in our suburban home surrounded by thousands of pounds of appliances, clothes, furniture, electronics; thousands of pounds of stuff to entertain us and protect us and keep us comfortable. Now, all we have is what's in our packs—and an overwhelming sense of space and freedom.

—Dan's journal

Our first campsite is a patch of flat dirt a few yards off the trail, a space barely large enough for our ground cloth and air mattresses. We don't bother with the tarp: rain on a night like this is about as likely as finding the Publishers' Clearinghouse prize patrol waiting for us at the next road crossing. We cook dinner, being careful to reuse our macaroni water for hot chocolate, then lounge on our sleeping pads and watch the shadows creep across the valleys. Low voices float on the breeze—other thru-hikers! Who else could they be?

Oak tree, San Jose Del Valle

Who else indeed—since the shadowy forms aren't carrying backpacks, and the voices aren't speaking English. Along the trail we've seen discarded tortilla wrappers, cardboard orange juice containers labeled in Spanish, and rusting cans that once held refried beans. The two men, small and dark, turn away from us and melt into the chaparral.

"Illegals" they are called; adjective turned noun. We've been warned about them by friends in San Diego, as well as by other hikers, the Pacific Crest Trail Association, and two ladies we met while walking through the border town of Campo. "They travel in packs. Sometimes, 30 at a time. They've got knives. They'll take your food, your water, your gear."

We've heard these kinds of well-intentioned warnings on other hikes. There's always some reason not to go into the wilderness: grizzly bears, rattlesnakes, snowstorms, heat, cold, the Indians on the reservation, the rednecks in the next county. Not that I discount the warnings; I don't. Where there's smoke there's fire, and all that. It's just that sometimes, it's only a teeny little cook-fire, not a three-engine conflagration.

Anyway, I have an inbred sympathy for people who slip under a fence hoping for a better life, because nearly 50 years ago, my father was one of them. His situation was different: for one thing, the communist guards along the Czech-German border were trying to keep him in, not shut him out. But as he crawled through the forests carrying some dried mushrooms for food, I don't think he looked or felt much different than the two men we see creeping past our camp. Come to think of it, they don't look too different from Dan and me, except, of course, for our clutter of bright-colored high-tech hiking equipment, which probably cost more money than these men have seen in their lives. For all that, we're no less dirty, smelly, tired, and sunburnt.

A sense of whimsy makes me wonder what the would-be immigrants would have to say had they stopped to record their thoughts in the trail register back at the border monument. Despite the vast differences between our journeys, I can't help but suppose that their reflections would be similar to ours. Perhaps they would write about hope and uncertainty, knowing—as do we—that only a lucky few will succeed. Perhaps they would wonder about the choice they made to come here, or ponder the dangers ahead and the promise of a new life whose rules and customs they do not yet know. Perhaps, if they signed the register, they would find the words that eluded me.

Later, as a shroud of dusk chills the air and the sun loiters over the western horizon, two Immigration and Naturalization Service helicopters come, hunting. Swooping down in tandem, they linger for a moment above our campsite before determining that we're not who they are looking for. Then they roar away. I feel an inexplicable relief as silence returns to the ridges.

Darkness descends, creeps down the hillsides. The night stills; the sky blackens. Somewhere, I once read that some 60,000 stars are visible to the human eye. All 60,000 of them must be out tonight, not counting the thick, chalky swath of the Milky Way, flinging a million universes heavenward. Low on the horizon lies Polaris. It is not the brightest star in the sky, but my eyes keep returning to it. From now on, it will be our personal beacon, our constant companion. For the next five months we will follow it north.

In the interest of honesty I have to pause a moment to admit that all this grandiose talk of five months and 2,600 miles and six million steps—all these big, unfathomable numbers—is a little misleading, at least as it applies to our everyday hiking life. The truth is, you can't walk across the country—or at least, I can't walk across the country—thinking only of the big numbers that separate the beginning from the end. If the goal were merely to get to Canada, we'd be better off taking a bus.

Granted, we're more than willing to hold court with anyone who happens to ask where we're going. "Canada," we tell them, and revel in their disbelief, their questions, their fleeting, flattering attention.

But in reality, Canada might as well be Valhalla, so seemingly unreachable, so infinitely faraway as it seems. The issues that occupy our thoughts are much more mundane: hot spots on our feet, rashes under our pack belts. Our daily goals, too, are modest: the next spring, the next shady lunch spot, the next good campsite. But—the call of the wild notwithstanding—as an incentive to walk more miles faster, nothing compares to the prospect of taking a break in town.

Ironic, isn't it? Here we are, such gung-ho outdoorspeople, and we're racing to town, hoping there's a motel. Shouldn't we be satisfied with putting up our tent in a Forest Service campground and taking our bath in the Freezy Fork of the Glacier River?

Well, to claim credit where it's due, I've taken plenty of baths in the good old Freezy Fork, and been glad of them, too. Same goes for Forest Service campgrounds, especially when they come equipped with such luxuries as garbage pick-up (so we don't have to pack out our trash) and running water (we can give our filter a rest).

But if I've got to plead guilty to wimpdom, I'm happy to do it: three days and 43 miles into our trip, I am unabashedly delighted to reach the road to Mount Laguna, a tiny resort community, nestled at 6,000 feet and surrounded by sweet-smelling forests of Jeffrey pines.

For one thing, there's the startling change in environment. First, there are trees, casting deep pools of shade as refreshing as a mid-summer swimming hole. And there is color: yellow violets and purple irises carpet the forest floor. By virtue of a 3,500-foot gain of elevation, we have climbed out of the semi-desert chaparral into the transition zone, the ecological equivalent of walking 600 miles north. It's colder up here—also wetter. The Lagunas steal moisture from eastward-moving Pacific clouds by forcing the wet ocean air to rise. As the air rises it cools; as it cools it precipitates on the mountains. Snow in this area sometimes falls late into the spring. Early-season thru-hikers frequently find themselves post-holing in thigh-deep drifts while just east of the mountains—but nearly a vertical mile below—the Colorado Desert broils in the Laguna's rain shadow, a parched dun wasteland subsisting on as little as 2 measly inches of annual precipitation.

But even more compelling is the prospect of amenities unavailable on the trail. Mount Laguna doesn't have much, but it does boast a lodge, a general store, a restaurant with limited hours and a more limited menu, and, most important, a post office where—we hope—the boxes of food and supplies we packed and shipped to ourselves in advance are waiting.

The clerk who answers the night bell is used to hikers straggling in at all hours.

"You look in better shape than the last two that came in," she observes. "One of them could hardly walk. I put them in the closest room so they wouldn't have to limp to the other end of the lodge."

We've met the hikers she's talking about. Brent and Roger are recent college graduates who blasted past us on the trail. They covered 20 miles by early afternoon their first day out, and did the whole 43-mile stretch from the border to Mount Laguna in just two days. They are stereotypical of PCT thru-hikers: young men in their twenties with muscles made of iron and confidence to match. Fit, fast, and eager like puppies, they make me feel a thousand years old. I am in awe of their strength and their speed, but I don't envy Brent his feet, which are paying the price of his gang-buster start: they are covered in blisters. His gait resembles that of someone walking barefoot across a bed of nails.

The clerk has seen it all before: "There's always something," she says. People quit the hike right here—just up and pay somebody local a hundred bucks to drive them back to San Diego. Or they limp in sick from heat and dehydration, or they have had their stuff stolen by the "illegals." Mostly it's blisters, the bane of the break-in days, when tender feet sizzle, swell, and sweat with virtually every step.

Inside the hotel room, luxury reigns—our definition of luxury being anything that we don't have on the trail: shade from the sun, air conditioning, sheets. No matter that the restaurant isn't open for breakfast—we can cook eggs from the lodge store on our camp stove. Or that there is no laundromat. I pile our dirty clothes into the sink and call Dan into the bathroom so that he, too, can admire the rinse water, which is the exact color of coffee—French Roast, no milk. But for sheer, awe-inspiring, profligate luxury, nothing compares to the shower itself. I turn on the faucet and step inside and feel the foreign sensation of water on skin, and I stand there as streaks of brown and gray run off my body, and I let the water run, and run, and run.

The next day, we tend to our resupply. These food drops are the crux of the how-to of long-distance backpacking. On average, hikers carry about a week's worth of food at a time, which means that about once every 100 to 150 miles, we've got to leave the trail to resupply. Unfortunately, small-town general stores don't tend to stock the kind of supplies hikers need. Over the last several months, Dan and I have bought and packed every item of nonperishable food we expect to consume in the next half-year, as well as consumable supplies like toothpaste, mosquito repellent, sunscreen, socks, laundry detergent, and film. We have 27 resupply stops. The shortest distance between them is 50 miles; the longest, 200 miles.

The main criteria for food is that it be lightweight (that rules out 2-pound cans of beans), nonperishable (most fruit and vegetables are off-limits), and easily packable (no bulky breads that will get

Yucca blooming near Tule Springs, Cleveland National Forest

squashed in a pack). Some hikers opt for home-dehydrating, which provides inexpensive, nutritious meals (but at the price of hundreds of hours in the kitchen). More convenient, but expensive, are commercial freeze-dried foods. But despite the variety of delicious-sounding flavors—spicy Thai chicken, beef enchilada ranchero, shrimp Cantonese—many hikers find that a long-term freeze-dried diet gets monotonous and doesn't meet their nutritional needs. A third choice is grocery store fare, where you concoct your menu from commonly available packaged foods: mac and cheese, spaghetti, small cans of tuna, tomato sauce, instant rice, potatoes, cous-cous, and so on. Finally, health food and ethnic specialty stores offer a variety of instant noodle soups, sauces, and dips. Dan and I lean heavily (pun intended) toward grocery store fare, but if we're out more than five days, weight considerations take over and we start using freeze-dried food.

No matter what's in your pack, one constant applies: it's never enough. Long-distance hikers burn 4,000 to 6,000 calories a day. It's simply not possible to carry that much.

We collect our food boxes and sort supplies, dividing food by meals, and counting to make sure we have the right number of breakfasts, lunches, and dinners, as well as trail mix and Snickers bars and powdered drinks. We get rid of coffee (a diuretic) and replace it with powdered Gatorade (electrolyte replacement), and we check our first aid supplies to be sure we have enough ointments and painkillers to take care of heat rashes and muscle aches until we reach the next oasis.

When we've finished our chores, we hang out at the lodge with Brent and Roger and read the register to see who's ahead of us. Another hiker, named Tom, wanders in, carrying an umbrella. Introductions are casual: in the long-distance hiking community, it's possible to walk with someone for hundreds of miles and not know his or her last name or occupation. Sometimes—because hikers often use trail handles—you don't even know a fellow hiker's first name. On more than one occasion, I've answered the telephone to find a confused operator asking if I'd accept a collect call from someone named Stinko or Ratman. Tom's trail name is Scribe, earned on the Appalachian Trail because he wrote a weekly column about his hike for a local newspaper.

The talk follows a wholly predictable arc: blisters, the heat, gear, the heat, how to minimize pack weight, the heat, does an umbrella really work as sun protection, the heat, food, the heat. And then it turns to snow. It seems ludicrous to be fretting about snow at this particular moment, but this past winter was especially snowy in parts of California and most of the Pacific Northwest; we've all heard rumors of impassable passes and 20-foot accumulations in the Sierra. Here in the dry-lands of southern California, the trail will shortly rise to elevations above 8,000 feet, so the conversation isn't as absurd as it seems—nor are the ice axes that some of the hikers are carrying. Still, there's no question that both the conversation and the ice axes are at least a couple of weeks premature: leaving Mount Laguna, the trail heads 4,000 feet downhill into the tangle of badlands, plains, and steep canyons that is the Anza-Borrego Desert.

Like any other married couple, Dan and I have between us several non-resolvable permanent differences. For the most part, we take the "you do it your way; I'll do it mine" approach, which works reasonably well in everyday life when we can indulge our tendencies to work autonomously.

This independent-minded *laissez faire* goes out the window on a thru-hike. As hiking partners, Dan and I have to agree on every decision of consequence: how far to walk, how many days of food to carry, when to stop for breaks, when to eat which meals, and—most important at the moment— when to get up in the morning. Virtually every hike we've ever been on begins with the great wakeup-call debate. As far as Dan is concerned, there is no such thing as too early. I, on the other hand, am an incorrigible night owl whose biological rhythms rightfully belong to a resident of a time zone in Mongolia. It's not that I don't agree that 6:00 A.M. is a lovely time of day—I do. I'd just rather stay up for it than get up for it.

It's a measure of just how hot it is that on this hike, Dan doesn't even have to raise the issue: I'm the one who suggests we start walking at first light, which means up at four-thirty, on the trail by five. Dan looks at me and says, "Who are you and what have you done with my wife?"

But if Dan wins (if by default) the get-up-in-the-morning battle, I score points (also by default) on the how-long-do-we-break-for-lunch decision. With a 5:00 A.M. start, we can easily cover 10 or 12 miles by ten in the morning. Since it doesn't get dark until well past nine at night, we can cover another 8 to 10 miles in the late afternoon. Which means that we can sit out the heat of the day and still get in our 20 miles.

On the shoulder of Palmview Peak, San Bernardino National Forest

View of Palm Springs from Apache Springs camp, San Bernardino National Forest

Tahquitz Peak, San Jacinto Wilderness

Looking west from the Trail, San Jacinto Wilderness

The theory gets put to the test two days after we leave Mount Laguna, as we approach the shoulder of Grapevine Mountain on the edge of the Anza-Borrego Desert on a stretch of trail our guidebook calls "a truly dangerous, waterless, desert path." Those are the adjectives; here are the facts:

- 24 miles between water sources.
- 2,000 feet of elevation gain.
- 100 degree temperatures—in the shade.
- There is no shade.

May 11. Day 6. Mile 78. Scissor's Crossing, Anza-Borrego Desert.

Life is reduced to water. Needing it, planning for it, thinking about it, finding it, drinking it. Some sympathetic soul put a couple of 5-gallon jugs of water on the side of the trail with a note telling hikers to drink up. What magic! The five of us—Karen and me, plus Brent, Roger, and Tom—seem to have formed an informal little traveling group. We are camped off the side of a highway under a cottonwood that looks much too big to be able to make a life for itself off the tiny trickle of murky water that is San Felipe Creek. Nonetheless, water it is. Considering what lies ahead, I think we'll be looking back at this muddy puddle quite sentimentally by this time tomorrow.

—DAN'S JOURNAL

Of California's 100 million acres, about 28 percent are desert, broadly classified as sparsely vegetated regions of less than 10 inches of annual rainfall. Within this definition, however, California has three distinct desert environments, differentiated primarily by elevation. The hottest and driest is the lower Sonora zone, which lies below 2,000 feet in elevation and may receive as little as 2 inches of annual precipitation. The upper Sonora zone, found in the Mojave, lies between 2,000 and 5,000 feet and is middling in both temperature and elevation. And the Great Basin is—at least by desert standards—high (above 4,000 feet) and cold. The Pacific Crest Trail goes through all three of them.

Thru-hikers frequently describe all of southern California's PCT as desert. This is understandable from a hiker's point of view: hikers are mostly concerned about heat and water, and during the PCT hiking season, virtually all of southern California has far too much of one and nowhere near enough of the other. More accurately, however, the PCT spends most of its time in southern California in a semi-desert environment of chaparral, on mountain slopes which, because of the rain-catching effect of elevation, receive more annual precipitation than the desert valleys. For the most part, the trail descends to the scorched lowlands only when necessary, grazing and recoiling from them like a hand touching a hot oven.

Here, in the San Felipe Hills, the trail has no choice but to enter the inferno. As it was originally proposed, the trail didn't go anywhere near this lair of lizards and refuge of rattlesnakes; it was supposed to be routed through the greener, cooler, rain-catching Volcan Mountains on the western side of the San Felipe Valley. But trail organizers were unable to negotiate easements through the private property there. Thus we find ourselves racing the sun as we climb Grapevine Mountain, following the trail as it wends its way through tangles of agave and creosote, prickly assortments of jumping cholla, barrel, and pin-cushion cactus, and bizarre forests of bare-branched ocotillo.

As we traverse the slopes of Grapevine Mountain, the first rays of morning sun are hitting the ridges above us. The line of shade creeps down the hillsides, inexorably imminent. Slowly, the temperature rises.

By nine o'clock, we have walked 9 miles. Our thermometer reads 100 degrees. The heat shimmers in lazy waves. The trail contours above a flat plain dotted with scrub oak. Scrub oak is not a good shade tree: the leaves are pointy and prickly and the branches grow close to the ground; it's hard to squeeze underneath. But in this scarcely vegetated landscape, the scrub oaks look as magisterial as sequoias. One of them casts an especially dense, dark shadow. The temptation proves impossible to resist. We cut cross-country toward the tree and come upon a rattlesnake going in the same direction, undoubtedly with the same idea. He ignores us and, in a little while, veers off to hide beneath a cactus.

Our patch of shade isn't big enough for all five of us. Brent and Roger squeeze under the tree. Tom, Dan, and I put up two tarps and lay our ground cloths underneath. The edge of the tarp's shadow separates us from the heat outside as decisively as would a wall. Crawling out into the sun is like stepping from an air-conditioned room into a sauna. By noon, the temperature under the tarp is 108 degrees. I don't know what the ground temperature is in the sun: my thermometer only goes up to 120. When Dan goes outside to cook, he uses Tom's umbrella for a sunshade. Even so, the heat hits him with the force of a linebacker in a full-body slam.

We have been on the trail for a week, but it seems like we have been walking forever. For entertainment, we browse through the guidebook—more accurately, a section of the guidebook. To save weight, we've torn the actual book into sections. New sections arrive as we need them in our food drops. In Volume I of the California guidebook, there are 18 sections, identified by letters from A–R. Volume II, which covers Oregon and Washington, is divided into 12 sections, labeled A–L. Brent points out that we are still in Volume I, Section A.

When it is no longer too hot to walk, we crawl out from under the tree. It is 10 minutes before 5:00. Dan notes that our lunch hour has lasted 7 hours and 40 minutes.

The Pacific Crest Trail is somewhat misnamed. There is no such thing as a Pacific Crest mountain range. There are the Cascades in Oregon and Washington and the Sierra Nevada of California; at one point, the PCT veers completely off-course and heads west into northern California's Klamath Range. South of the Sierra, the picture is even more confused, with a jumble of ranges mingled and mangled by the constant upheaval of the San Andreas fault. Nor is the PCT strictly a ridgeline trail. To the contrary, here in southern California, it ascends from the scorching desert valleys into so-called sky-islands: mountains separated from each other by surrounding seas of heat and sand.

"Our desert scenery is probably affected more by the presence of mountains than by any other geological feature," writes Edmund Jaeger in *The California Deserts*. "The monotony of pale-faced basins is everywhere broken by the stern but colorful peaks and massive ridges which protrude islandlike from the vast sea of sand and gravel."

Twelve days into our hike, the San Jacintos are our first major range: the first time we will ascend into the boreal zones above 8,000 feet; the first time we will breathe thin air; the first time we will step on snow.

The climb is not easy. What we've learned so far about the PCT is that the footway is almost always well-graded and it doesn't tend to be exceedingly steep, but the climbs can go on for many miles at a time. Beginning at an elevation of 3,990 feet at our resupply stop at the Kamp Anza Kampground, our route ascends nearly a vertical mile to an apex of 9,030 feet. The actual elevation gain is even more, because the route follows a roller-coaster course of fits and starts: 1,000 feet of climbing followed by 500 feet of descending; 2,000 feet up, 1,000 down, and so on and so forth, up and down over dry crumbly granite, in and out of countless ravines, around cliffs and outcroppings, into shady canyons lined with Coulter pines and live oaks, and up to xeric ridges of scrubby sunburnt shrubs.

The full climb is a two-day affair: we don't reach the high point until the middle of the second day. But finally, we are on the crest, shaded first by white firs and spruce, then by cool, lofty lodgepoles. Now the PCT lives up to its name, riding the ridgeline on top of the world. Little puddles of snowmelt trickle into seasonal streams, and an occasional, unbelievable patch of snow lingers on the shady side of the mountains. I feel like a native of some tropical island seeing snow for the first time. In the trickling path of the snowmelt, an unusual flower, stout and fleshy like a succulent, seizes this brief moment of plenty to sprout and bloom a brilliant red. I look it up and learn that it's called a snow plant. They sometimes grow right on the trail, but hikers ahead of us have surrounded them with protective little rock piles, a reminder for us to tread lightly. I like the rock walls: they show respect. Anything that lives here deserves it.

Prickly-pear cactus, Gold Canyon

May 18. Day 13. Mile 182. San Jacinto Mountains.

Our campsite tonight is a flat spot barely big enough for a ground cloth. Our perch juts out over endless acres of pale golds and browns that seem to disappear into the dusty air. Smog, unfortunately. Up here, the air is clear—and surprisingly cold. We're at an elevation of 9,030, our highest to date. I am wearing polypropylene long johns and a balaclava and my rain jacket to keep out the wind. It seems unbelievable that only four hours ago, we were huddled under a tarp to escape from the sun.

—DAN'S JOURNAL

Hiking southern California is a little like following the bouncing path of a gigantic Superball. From our high camp in the San Jacintos, the trail heads down to 1,190 feet—that's a loss of a vertical mile and a half. The distance between water sources is 25 miles and 7,600 feet. Even for a northbound hiker going downhill, these numbers are ridiculous. I cannot imagine how anyone could ever hike this trail in the other direction.

Then again, what goes down must come up: an eternity below us the thin ribbon of Interstate 10 runs through San Gorgonio Pass. On the other side of the pass rises our future: the San Bernardino Mountains, where we will in short order regain all the elevation we are currently losing. Looking from the bottom of the canyon to the top of the ridge, you can see all six of California's life zones, from lower Sonora desert to arctic-alpine tundra. Variations of rainfall and temperature account for almost 250 species of plants, including incense cedars and white firs, and Coulter, Jeffrey, ponderosa, sugar, lodgepole, and limber pines.

Descending, I find myself wishing for a bridge from mountaintop to mountain-top. Or wings. The trail lurches and sways like a drunken sailor. It climbs up, over, and around Fuller Ridge on rotten, tortuous footway, then descends the north slope of the San Jacinto Mountains, a stark escarpment sculpted by the San Andreas Fault, then scoured and scarred by avalanches. In shaded northern crevasses, snow still clings to the cliffs. John Muir, who knew something about such things, called it, "the most sublime spectacle to be found anywhere on this earth."

As we descend, the temperature rises, about 5 degrees each time we drop 1,000 feet. Far faster than we climbed above the shadeless shrubs we descend back into them.

But no matter how long we walk, the highway remains in fixed position, infinitely far away. We swing above it, ducking in and out of dry gullies and around spur ridges, zigging and zagging until I feel dizzily disoriented. Below us a police helicopter buzzes back and forth over the interstate, on speeding-ticket duty. It looks as small and insignificant as a mosquito. Its drone is as annoying.

Above us, something so unusual is happening that we must look twice to be sure. Clouds the color of bruises are gathering. "Incoming rain clouds are generally for me the signal to start desertward," writes Jaeger in *The California Deserts*. "Let me have the delicious odors of the creosote bush and the saltbush when they are wetted by gentle rains, look upon the endless variety and beauty of the clouds' far-flung forms, have the silence of the uninhabited mesa, and I am in a land enchanted."

The clouds look as out of place as a thru-hiker at a formal dinner party. They get on with their business and are finished in no time. Within 15 minutes, they have managed to build, then they blitz down the mountainside flinging beneath them a purple curtain of rain. We are not in the path of the storm, but when we cross it an hour or so later, all that is left are a few puddles of water that are evaporating as quickly as they arrived. The smell of the wet desert is sharply pungent, like freshly ground spice.

We have reached the point in our hike where such things as the smell of the wet desert and the color of the flowers take up more space in our brains than the everyday physical challenges. Now, as we knew they would, the challenges have become routine.

The climb from Interstate 10 at San Gorgonio Pass (elevation 1,200 feet) to the ridge of the San Bernardino Mountains (8,600 feet) is longer than any other northbound climb on the entire PCT. I am surprised to find myself climbing easily. My body is no longer clunking and creaking like a decrepit old car that's spent the last three decades in somebody's barn. I wouldn't go so far as to call myself a well-oiled machine, but a little self-congratulation seems in order. I can get from the bottom of a mountain to the top without whining or even wanting to. My pack feels like an old friend on my back. The heat is no longer a stranger. Even the territorial rattlesnakes seem par for the course.

Brent and Roger have pulled ahead of us. Another hiker, a soft-spoken ex-Marine master sergeant named Steve, has hooked up with Tom. The four of us have been loosely keeping pace with each other. I find that I enjoy walking along with new companions, having the kind of all-day conversations I haven't had time for since college. The difference is that on the trail, there's a much broader spectrum of people —all occupations, all ages. Steve, for instance, fought in Vietnam and was a guard on Marine I, the presidential helicopter. He says that hiking the PCT is the biggest challenge he's ever undertaken.

Just now, however—having earned the ridge of the San Gabriels—the trail is more gentle than challenging, often shaded and rarely climbing more than 500 feet at a time. The hiking is fast and easy. Ahead of us the town of Big Bear beckons, where we are planning two full days of R and R to celebrate my 38th birthday. A friend of ours says that thru-hiking adds five years to your life; therefore the secret to immortality is to hike a long trail every five years.

NON-POTABLE
WATER
FOR HORSES ONLY

DAN GETTING WATER

May 25. Day 20. Mile 276. Big Bear City.

This is our first major town stop, so it's a good time to take stock. Our bodies, our spirits, and our gear are all holding up well. So far, we've averaged 15 miles a day, including our days off. Actual walking mileage has been climbing up to 20 a day; it needs to stay there for us to do a single-season thru-hike.

—DAN'S JOURNAL

Long-distance desert hiking sometimes seems a series of sprints from one oasis to the next. Usually, the towns are the places to rest and replenish, but sometimes the trail has a few tricks up its sleeve. Thirty-three miles north of Big Bear is an oasis so pretty and peaceful it might well be the original Garden of Eden.

It has a hot spring—and not only a hot spring, but a landscaped series of rock pools and terraces that catch the hot water running off the side of the hill. Each pool is big enough for a small group of bathers. When you get too hot from the spring water, you can slide into cold Deep Creek and float past cattails and willows in water so clear you can see your toes when you stand. The fish are jumping, and, were there any cotton, I am certain it would be high.

If I could stop time here, I would. Lying first in the hot pool, then in the cold creek, then back again in the pool, I feel the sort of well-being you might have sitting by your fire on a snowy winter night with a glass of red wine, a good book, and Mozart on the stereo. I could spend a week here. Maybe someday, I will simply show up with my tent and a book and nothing to do but ease myself in and out of the water.

But now is not the time for that kind of indolence. I can spend an hour but not a day—and certainly not a week. It's the mantra of a thru-hike: We must keep moving. So we do.

And the trail, being what it is, goes back to being what it was. It heads down into sunshine and scrub, drops past the sluggish waters of the land-locked Mojave River (which evaporates long before it ever reaches the sea), and deposits us back among the territorial rattlesnakes, the ubiquitous cacti, and the shadeless chaparral. Perhaps it's the big mileage we're doing—68 miles in three days; maybe it's the pesky ache that seems to have settled in my feet (commenting, no doubt, on the mileage). Perhaps it's the heat, which has resumed now that the trail is back to its old ornery self. Whatever the reason, as we begin yet another endless descent into yet another pass from which we will ascend to yet another mountain range, I find myself suddenly and completely enervated, as though the sun has drained away all the energy in my body. It feels like my muscles are made of wet noodles, my blood made of water.

Oases exist in the present and the future, not the past. Deep Creek is now only a faded memory; our immediate reality is the familiar heat and thirst, the long dusty traverses. Ahead of us Cajon Pass and Interstate 15 lure us to walk through the midday heat with the promise, the possibility, the prayer that somewhere in the dusty canyon there will be respite—a hotel, a restaurant, a 7-11… I'll even take a cement culvert if it will get the sun off my skin.

View of Mount San Jacinto from Gold Canyon

Cajon Pass, glory be, has all of the above, culvert included. At Tiffany's restaurant, we catch up with Tom and Steve, who left Big Bear a day ahead of us. They are trying, so far unsuccessfully, to summon up the will to go back out into the blistering heat. The waitress doesn't even blink at our disheveled appearance; she's used to stinking apparitions who crawl in croaking, "Water, water." Before we've even slumped into our chairs, she's got a pitcher of water on the table and another one on its way.

The four of us trade notes—who's ahead, who's behind, who's doing what, what's ahead. For the next section, the trail frankly goes psychotic. Even the irrepressible John Muir was taken aback by the San Gabriel Mountains: "The whole range, seen from the plain, with the hot sun beating upon its southern slopes, wears a terribly forbidding aspect."

Forbidding indeed. The next 25 miles are completely waterless. Not only that, but they involve climbing 5,300 feet, then descending (for purposes of resupply) 2,500 feet on a side-trail to the town of Wrightwood. Tom and Steve have declared that this makes no sense, and have decided instead to walk along a highway that goes directly into Wrightwood in less than half the distance without climbing the equivalent of four Empire State Buildings.

Dan and I are taking the trail. I can't really say why. It's not like we're purists about such things. I just don't much care for the idea of walking along the shoulder of high-speed highways.

At any rate, we're heading up. But that's tomorrow's problem. Today, we're motel-bound.

We hope. At the motel, there is no sign of life. The door to the office is locked. No one is on duty behind the bullet-proof night window. A washing machine and dryer sit outside under an awning, covered with a layer of dust. There are no cars in the parking lot. The swimming pool is full of stagnant water. Tumbleweeds roll across the property like bit players in a movie about the effects of biological warfare on a small western town.

But the clerk materializes and gives us a room, the laundry machines are actually working, there is air conditioning, and wonder of wonders, a bathtub, which I immediately fill with ice-cold water. By 7:15, we are both sound asleep.

The next morning, it is still dark when we awaken just after four o'clock and head out to the steep south face of the San Gabriel Range with 15 liters of water sloshing in our packs.

Muir again:

> *In the mountains of San Gabriel . . . Mother Nature is most ruggedly, thornily savage. Not even in the Sierra have I ever made the acquaintance of mountains more rigidly inaccessible. The slopes are exceptionally steep and insecure to the foot of the explorer, however great his strength or skill may be, but thorny chaparral constitutes their chief defense. With [little] exception, the entire surface is covered with it, from the highest peak to the plain . . . From base to summit all seems gray, barren, silent-dead, bleached bones of mountains, overgrown with scrubby bushes, like gray moss.*

Well, it hasn't changed much. Not that there's anything new about Mother Nature being thornily savage. As far as the chaparral is concerned, we've been wading through the stuff since the Mexican border 330 miles back: it's the most common plant community on California's Pacific Crest Trail.

On the way uphill, a little interpretive nature trail identifies some of the rugged, ubiquitous plants.

It's not just the chaparral that give the San Gabriels their forbidding aspect. The steep south slopes remind us of the stark northern precipices of the San Jacintos, and for good reason: both were cut and shaped—are being cut and shaped—by the San Andreas Fault, which, along with its 10 associated tributary faults, is responsible for much of the jumbled, jagged topography of southern California's mountain ranges. The fault system moves horizontally—think of the Titanic grinding against the iceberg—and carries matter along the fault lines. At Cajon Pass, for instance, the conspicuous rock formations known as Mormon Rocks came from a place 25 miles to the southeast.

The fault system also produced three major passes known as interior gateways, two of which —San Gorgonio Pass and Cajon Pass—are on the Pacific Crest Trail. These interior gateways have been important transportation arteries since the earliest days of European exploration and settlement in California. As we cross the pass, I'm trying to imagine what it would have looked like a couple of

Big Bear Lake, San Bernardino National Forest

Silverwood Lake, San Bernardino National Forest

Sunset from Mount Baden-Powell, Sheep Mountain Wilderness

Limber pine atop Mount Baden-Powell, Sheep Mountain Wilderness

hundred years ago when the biggest Spanish overland expedition ever mounted in the New World crossed between the San Bernardino and San Gabriel mountains here at Cajon Pass. Captain Juan Bautista de Anza and 240 settlers were on their way to settle what would become San Francisco; the journey would cover 1,800 miles in 12 months. (Not fast by thru-hiker standards, but then again we have a trail and we know where we're going.)

The landscape must have looked much the same then as now. True, today there are the interstate and the railroad, but against the raw backdrop of the mountains, they look impermanent, insignificant. One thing has changed: the distance between San Francisco and Los Angeles. The San Andreas Fault has been moving matter at an average of 2 inches a year. Were de Anza to return today, his journey would be shorter by a distance of 34 feet.

The climb is every bit as tough and long and hot and thirsty as we expected, but the reward at the top is the Angeles Crest, one of southern California's premiere mountain landscapes. Here, two days later, we reach our highest point yet, at the windswept summit of 9,399-foot Mount Baden-Powell, named after the founder of the Boy Scouts. For a while, the PCT is contiguous with the Boy Scouts' Silver Moccasin Trail, and at irregular intervals on the way to the summit, the Scouts have erected trail markers that note the exact mileage (to the hundredth of a mile), and elevation (to the nearest foot). Dan and I amuse ourselves by guessing what each post will say; after nearly 400 miles on the trail, we find that we've become remarkably accurate.

At this elevation, we are in the so-called Canadian life zone, characterized by lodgepole pines and mixed firs. At the top of Baden-Powell, we make a rare foray into the even-higher Hudsonian zone where twisted, hulking, wind-battered limber pines preside. Some of them are thought to be 2,000 years old.

I have to admit that I've never been able to learn tree identification from a book. Somewhere between counting which needles go which way, what leaves have which kinds of lobes, or what cones have which barbs, my eyes glaze over. But there are other ways to learn. Walking through a forest at 2 or 3 miles an hour provides plenty of time for arboreal introductions. So does spending a couple of hours huddled in a patch of shade. At such times, trees quickly become good friends.

So I know cottonwoods, first of all, because they promise a drink of water. And live oaks, because their shade is so dense. I know aspens, because I can never pass an autumnal grove of aspen without wanting to stand inside their streaming golden light. I know straightforward, straight-up lodgepoles, because they mean I've reached cooler mountain climes, and because I like to lie beneath them and let them draw my eyes to the sky. Also: Coulter pines because their football-sized cones are so improbable; Jeffrey pines, because their bark smells of butterscotch; Western redcedars, because they are so ridiculously, unbelievably big; foxtail pines because they are so ridiculously, unbelievably twisted. And most of all, the denizens of the high country: krummholtz, the crooked little spruce that stubbornly grow where no trees should, and Limber pines, because they not only survive, but thrive on cold windy slopes where no other trees dare to live. These are trees with character, and strength, and will—the qualities a thru-hiker most needs, and admires.

At home, when Dan and I would fill in the sentence "I am _____" we would fill in the blank with our jobs: a writer, a teacher. Others might turn to other aspects of their lives: happy, depressed, an alcoholic, a success. Out here, we're thru-hikers.

Except that just now my right foot decides that it no longer wants anything to do with the business of thru-hiking.

At first, I think the pain is merely the continuation of a low-grade running argument that my feet and boots have been waging since the beginning of the hike. But these aren't the usual aches and pains of long-distance hiking. Nor is the problem due to blisters. (Despite my prehike sloth, I did obey the first commandment of backpacking: "Thou shalt not start the trail with untried boots.") The pain is a penetrating, intense ache inside my right heel; it feels centered in the very bones of my foot. I am popping Advil like M&Ms, but nothing works; nothing even helps except—ironically—walking, which numbs the pain. Too bad I can't walk all night, because the pain won't let me sleep. By the time we descend from the crest of

EVEN SOME GNARLED TREE STUMPS CAN PROVIDE A LITTLE SHADE

the San Gabriel Mountains into an R.V. campground in Soledad Canyon four days later, there is no doubt that I have to leave the trail to see a doctor.

Easier said than done. Our next food drop is only a few miles farther, but the town of Agua Dulce is so small that it doesn't have a post office, let alone a doctor. Hikers receive their resupply boxes through UPS delivery to the Century 21 real estate office, whose owners are what the hiking community calls trail angels—people who help hikers for no reason other than the satisfaction of taking part in their journey. Over the years, Dan and I have been the recipients of countless acts of trail magic. But if ever I have needed the help of a trail angel, it is now.

Joan Byrd and Bernice Canutt are the owners of the Century 21. Today, Joan is on duty. She is wearing a professional-looking ensemble that includes pumps, makeup, and pantyhose. By contrast, the four of us look like we've just escaped from the La Brea tar pits. Joan tells us to help ourselves to coffee and to feel free to use the restrooms, the Internet, and the telephone.

Dan digs through a pile of about 75 boxes piled up near the front of the office and retrieves ours, which he takes outside. I hit the yellow pages and the telephones in search of a doctor. The best I can do is a clinic in a not-so-nearby town where a physician's assistant will see me. Joan, who has a business meeting in the afternoon, offers to find someone to drive me. "Go ahead and make your appointment," she says. "I don't know how we'll get you there, but we will. You just have to trust me on this."

Which I do.

Sure enough, five minutes later, I'm on the phone with Peg Spry, an officer of a church up the road. Peg agrees to take me to the clinic in the afternoon; she also tells us that hikers can stay overnight in a back room at the church.

While I'm waiting for afternoon to come, Joan and I chat about the local real estate market, which is slow, and the properties, which are expensive. I ask about one particular house, a mansion atop a hill surrounded by so much grass it looks like the Emerald City. Even in wealthy horse-country, that much grass stands out; Joan knows immediately which property I mean.

"A property like that might go for a million dollars," she tells me.

I look around. Dan is sitting outside, in need of a shower and a shave, surrounded by the contents of three boxes of supplies that have managed to explode all over the sidewalk. I've filled an entire desk with papers and phone books. We are all on best behavior—Tom and Steve have even organized the boxes into piles and are starting to clean out the hiker grab box. But I'm thinking that a potential buyer of a million-dollar house isn't going to be someone who routinely does business surrounded by 75 boxes, four hikers who look like escapees from a chain gang, piles of freeze-dried food, and the wafting stink of eau-de-trail.

"What if someone came in right now and wanted to look at a house like that?" I ask.

Joan doesn't even understand the question.

"Well, we'd just ask you to answer the phones and we'd go out and show it to them," she says.

Here, the story gets convoluted. The clinic is miles away in one direction, the nearest pharmacy is as far away in the other direction. There's an orthopedic specialist to see, a health plan to argue with, a rental car (in yet another town) to obtain, and 300 miles of driving to do. So let me save all of us the hassle; let's just jump to the bottom line, which appears in the gray glow of an x-ray screen.

A fragmented piece of bone about the size of my thumbnail is sticking out of the bottom of my heel bone. Every time I step down, the weight of me and my pack smashes against this bone spur, which causes inflammation in the surrounding tissue. The doctor prescribes anti-inflammatories, gives me little rubber heel cups, and recommends different boots. This problem, he tells me, affects people differently. He thinks that if I take a few days off to let the inflammation go down, I can try to hike again. He does not, however, think I will be able to finish the entire trail. "The pain will tell you when it's time to stop," he says. When, not if.

It feels as if I've been fired from a job. You know: you're cruising along, doing your best, thinking everything is just fine and—bam!—the world is suddenly upside down. You just sit there with your head spinning.

Juniper berries, Vasquez Rocks County Park

Joshua trees in morning light, Mojave Desert

A jumble of discussions later, Dan and I settle on a plan. Dan will continue hiking with Tom and Steve as far as our next resupply in Mojave. After that, it's up to my foot: if I can, I'll rejoin the guys around Mojave and, if all goes well, I'll continue into the High Sierra. If not—well, we'll climb that pass when we come to it. We've been talking about pack horses or llamas. Maybe I could skip the Sierra, which I've hiked twice already, and rejoin Dan in a month or so.

June 6. Day 32. Mile 477. San Franciscito Ranger Station.

Mostly I'm wondering what will happen next. Can Karen continue, and if so, for how far? And if she can't, will I? So much has gone into this walk—half a year of planning and anticipation, not to mention the actual walking we've already done. When I'm hiking, all of the permutations are going through my mind. It's a good way to pass time, I guess, but not such a good way to enjoy the desert. One thing is for certain: she can't go into the Sierra unless we're sure her foot can handle it.

—Dan's Journal

The stretch of trail I'm skipping is one of the most controversial on the entire PCT. It illustrates one of the major challenges of putting a long-distance hiking trail on the ground: achieving a continuous border-to-border route. Across public land (which comprises 90 percent of the PCT's route) there's no problem, but to cross private land, trails need an easement. Unfortunately, trails can be convenient targets for local politicians in search of a government project whipping boy to rouse the rabble with. The objections become depressingly familiar: hikers will upset the cattle, leave gates open, start fires, spread diseases, let their dogs run loose, litter, and generally make a mess of things. Some landowners refuse to have anything to do with trails, easements, hikers, or anything else that smells like big government and environmentalists.

The Tehachapi Mountains form the southernmost extension of the Sierra Nevada. The proposed route would have crossed land owned by the giant, corporate-owned Tejon Ranch, which for years resisted the PCT with a fervor usually reserved for opponents more menacing than a simple hiking trail. The ranch became temporarily infamous in thru-hiker lore, with stories of armed guards allegedly patrolling the grounds and (again allegedly) shooting or threatening to shoot at hikers.

If the ranch had shotguns, the PCT organizers had tools of their own: the threat of condemnation, or taking a private property for public use. PCT officials have been loathe to use condemnation because it creates long-lasting bad feelings between land owners and the trail community. In this case, however, condemnation proceedings were set to start before an eleventh-hour compromise was reached. Not everyone, however, is enamored with the result. Our guidebook calls the new trail "a hot, waterless, dangerous, ugly, and entirely un-Crestlike segment of trail [that] now winds along a gerrymandered route [and]... entirely subverts Congress's vision of its greatest national scenic trail."

Dan does not believe in following sections of trail where the route is the result of political compromise. In our experience, such sections are of little attraction to hikers. So he (along with Steve and Tom) opts to take the former PCT route, which follows the Los Angeles aqueduct across the Antelope Valley and up Jawbone Canyon. In addition to going smack through the middle of a strange and wonderful, Joshua-tree-dotted landscape, this route has one other important feature: it's mostly accessible by some sort of road, so I can rent a car and camp with the guys at night. I can also bring them water.

Three days later, Dan rejoins the official route near Piñon Mountain. I use this time to give my foot the rest that the physician recommended, and then gingerly don my hiking boots and hoist my pack. When I rejoin Dan at Walker Pass, he is exuberant: we have left the desert behind, and now the high peaks are just ahead. As Dan descended into Walker Pass, he saw the High Sierra for the first time—a thin, jagged, sky-piercing line tipped in white.

How deep is the snow?

How will my foot hold out?

These are the questions that face us now, as we start the final, 50-mile stretch to Kennedy Meadows and the highcountry ahead.

Antelope Valley, Mojave Desert

Joshua trees near Walker Pass, Sequoia National Forest

View east from Mount Jenkins

Kern River, South Sierra Wilderness

chapter 2

THE HIGH SIERRA: ROCK AND ICE

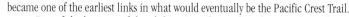

June 16. Day 42. Mile 699. Kennedy Meadows.

Kennedy Meadows looks like a cross between a Grateful Dead concert and an outdoor trade show. Some 50 thru-hikers have gathered here, preparing for the next leg of the journey. Everyone is in the process of counting food and checking equipment, making last minute decisions to carry or abandon something. The sense of anticipation tinged with fear reminds me of a team of climbers in the high camp the night before summit day. Or of a staging area for troops about to be helicoptered into combat. Check, recheck, check, recheck. Hikers who have never climbed before hold their ice axes as though they are some strange amulet that will protect them against evil. Rumors are rampant. Supposedly, the light rain that fell here last night was snow higher up. Some people have decided to skip the High Sierra because of snow; others, seemingly oblivious to it, are planning to wear sneakers and cover 25 miles a day. The truth is, no one knows what lies ahead.

—DAN'S JOURNAL

Three things make the High Sierra different from any other terrain on the Pacific Crest Trail.

First: The Sierra Nevada contains the longest continuous stretch of wilderness in the contiguous United States. By trail, the distance from Kennedy Meadows to Reds Meadow is 200 miles, and between the two, there is not a single road, not a single town, not even a power line.

Second: Within these 200 miles, the Pacific Crest Trail crosses nine passes whose elevations range from 10,900 to 13,180 feet. In June, when the thru-hikers arrive, most of these passes, and many miles of trail leading up to and down from them, are still covered with several feet of snow.

Third: June is the height of the Sierra snowmelt. Atop the peaks and passes, a winter's worth of snow is first melting, then trickling—then cascading, plunging, roaring—into dozens of creeks and rivers that thru-hikers must cross. Most of the crossings are unbridged.

John Muir wrote on the subject of hiking the length of the Sierra:

> *There are many ways across the range, old ways graded by glaciers and followed by men and bears, but not a single way, natural or artificial, has yet to be constructed along the range; and the traveler who will thus move in a direction at right angles to the course of the ancient ice-rivers must make a way across canyons and ridges laid side by side in endless succession, and all roughened with gorges, gulches, land-slips, precipices, and stubborn chaparral.*

In 1915, a year after Muir's death, the California legislature approved funding for a trail to run lengthwise along the range—that is, across those gorges, gulches, land-slips, and precipices—and named it after the grand old man himself. Construction was completed in 1931, and the John Muir Trail became one of the earliest links in what would eventually be the Pacific Crest Trail.

Part of the business of thru-hiking is understanding that you don't always get to traverse any particular place during its optimum season. In an average year, the High Sierra is snow-free only during July, August, and September (that's if you're lucky). Thru-hikers, true to form, arrive in June.

Dan and I have hiked the High Sierra before, five times between us, including on our honeymoon. But we have never crossed these formidable mountains during snowmelt. The difference is to the order of swimming 2,000 laps in a pool or swimming the same distance across the English Channel.

Further complicating the planning process is the fact that no two years are alike. To wit: the data book reports snow conditions along or near the trail in California. The snow-depth measurements are taken around April 1 of each year. At Piute Pass, which is close to the trail and has conditions similar to those found on the trail's high passes, the average annual snowfall over the 20-year period was 100 inches. Actual annual accumulations, however, ranged from 33 inches in 1977 to 185 inches in 1969. Clearly, people hiking the High Sierra in those two years had radically different experiences.

How does this affect thru-hikers? In 1994, Piute Pass had 71 inches of snow; the PCTA estimates that 40 of 75 potential thru-hikers finished their Mexico-to-Canada journey. In 1995, Piute Pass had 162 inches of snow and only 10 of 75 hikers finished. In 1996, it had 111 inches of snow (very close to an average year), and 60 of 100 hikers finished.

But the correlation is a little more complicated than that. In 1997, when we hiked, the winter snowfall was unusually heavy—all the way back in the chaparral country of the Mexican border, snow-depth was a topic of concern among hikers. But since then, the spring has been unusually warm and dry; word is that the snowpack is now sitting right at about average. But no one knows for sure.

There is no way that the gear we used for southern California's five climatic zones is going to be able to handle the sixth, appropriately called the arctic-alpine zone. Arctic-alpine means cold; also windy, sometimes snowy, and always exposed. It means stark, clean winds and air so crisp it practically crackles. It also means more weight in our packs: a tent instead of a tarp, warmer sleeping bags, extra layers of clothing, a bigger fuel bottle with more fuel in it, ice axes, topographic maps, and instep crampons. By the time we've finished sorting our gear, my svelte, trim desert pack has metamorphosed into one of those obese behemoths you see legendary sherpas hauling over the Himalayas.

Important difference here: no one has ever described me as a legendary sherpa.

So, having engaged in the time-honored thru-hiker tradition of gathering together all the gear we need for these new conditions, we turn to the equally time-honored tradition of reconsidering whether we really do need it all. We make piles of clothes, weigh the pluses and minuses of balaclavas versus hats and gloves versus mittens, calculate just exactly how much fuel do we need, examine the contents of our first-aid kit. When we start counting Band-Aids, we know that neurosis has gotten the best of us. At the end of the day we have managed to designate the following items as unnecessary:

1. Several bags and bottles for carrying water. (Carrying water is not something we have to worry about now that our primary challenge will be dealing with too much water in frozen or flowing form.)

View of Owens Lake, Golden Trout Wilderness

2. One 10-ounce water filter. (We figure that drinking snowmelt in the Sierra in June is pretty safe. We are, however, carrying a small bottle of iodine pills for cases where the water seems iffy, like lower elevations, meadows, algae-painted watermelon-pink snowfields, and so on.)

You don't need a postal scale to figure out that what we've added to our packs is a heck of a lot heavier than what we're sending away.

And that's not even counting food. Simple arithmetic tells us all we need to know. Figure 14 days to hike 200 miles plus one day to climb Mount Whitney (which, at 14,494 feet is the highest peak in the contiguous United States and not something most thru-hikers can walk past without climbing). Figure 2 pounds of food per person per day. The grand total of food alone: 60 pounds for the two of us.

Some hikers are planning to lower their food weight by hiking bigger mileage. (I keep hearing the words "25 miles a day" bandied about, although it seems inconceivable to me that anyone can cover that distance over a bunch of 12,000-foot snow-covered passes.) More reasonably, some hikers go off-trail to resupply. But here's the thing: resupplying means walking extra miles. Sometimes *a lot* of extra miles. And some of those miles involve multi-thousand foot ascents and descents.

More reasonable resupply options are offered by two backcountry lodges within a few miles of the trail, but they are so far north that using them only lightens your pack by a couple of days' worth of food. Dan argues that it isn't any more work to carry the extra food than to hike the extra miles, and when he says he's willing to carry the additional weight for both of us, I cheerfully agree.

Nonetheless, when I heft my pack at Kennedy Meadows, it feels as if an elephant has snuck inside. Dan's pack weighs about 65 pounds, which is heavy even for him. Mine is nearly 55 pounds, which is certainly heavy for me. Dan insists on looking on the bright side: he says his pack will only weigh 65 pounds until he eats the first candy bar. Since his pack is heavier, we eat his candy bars first.

The early miles are surprisingly easy. I have my sea legs now, you might say. My heel feels fine. My pack rides comfortably.

There is tremendous satisfaction in self-reliance; in having exactly what we need to travel through these mountains for the next 14 days. If we break something, we will have to fix it; if we lose something, we will have to improvise a substitute. Or do without. There is a giddy sense of liberation in knowing that even if we had a cell-phone (which we do not; no thank you, take your technology elsewhere) we couldn't use it: the mountains are too high, the distances too large.

I'm not someone who walks around with a head brimming with poetry, but a few lines of Walt Whitman come to mind:

> *Afoot and light hearted I take to the open road,*
> *Healthy, free, the world before me,*
> *The long brown path before me leading wherever I choose.*
> *Henceforth I ask not good fortune, I myself am good fortune . . .*
> *The earth, that is sufficient.*

A couple of hours into the walk, at a place called Beck's Meadow, the trees part, the view opens, and there they are, the mountains: high and steep and gleaming white. The shock stops us—stops my poetic musings, stops Dan's perennial, perpetual forward motion. I remember from our previous visits that the Sierra has this in-your-face quality. It makes no difference that I have seen the 5,000-foot canyons, the towering granite cirques, the sky-spearing pinnacles before. Frequently in the days ahead, I will have to stop walking and simply stand on the trail, waiting for my senses to catch up with me.

The word Sierra is often translated as mountain, but it more specifically refers to a range that is serrated, or sawtoothed. Nevada means snowy. In 1542, a Spanish ship captain, Juan Rodriquez Cabrillo, recorded seeing *una gran sierra nevada* to the east of Monterey. It was the coastal range, but the name Sierra Nevada stuck, and for the next 230 years, the term was used generically for mountain ranges on maps of California. It wasn't until 1772 that a Spanish expedition saw the mountains we today call the Sierra Nevada.

Weathered roots, Golden Trout Wilderness

Mount Whitney as seen from Crabtree Meadows, Inyo National Forest

Guitar Lake, Sequoia National Park

Mount Hitchcock, Sequoia National Park

View south from atop Mount Whitney, Sequoia National Park

A few more facts: running roughly 400 miles from Tehachapi Pass in the south to Mount Lassen in the north, the Sierra Nevada is the longest continuous mountain range in the 48 contiguous states. (The Appalachians and Rockies are subdivided into sub-ranges that have different geological histories.) The Sierra runs through three national parks, nine national forests, and one national monument; it contains the longest wilderness, deepest canyon, and highest mountain (again, in the contiguous states; Alaska, as usual, ruins the superlatives for everyone else). For PCT hikers, who can't fly like crows but must instead follow meandering up-and-down and round-the-mountain footpaths, it's about double the air distance—800 miles—from Tehachapi Pass to Lassen Volcanic National Park.

The general shape of the range is that of a tilted block of rock—think of a trapdoor propped just slightly ajar. The eastern escarpment is short (as little as 6 miles from base to summit), steep, and dramatic. Mount Whitney, for instance, looms 2.5 vertical miles over Death Valley's Badwater Canyon. By contrast, the western side of the range is gently sloped and sometimes as much as 60 miles wide. There is also asymmetry on the north-south axis; elevations are higher in the south than in the north.

The character of these mountains, with their jagged, fantastic pinnacles, nearly vertical walls, and scoured cirques, suggests a violent geological history. Indeed, early explorers and geologists used words like shock, trauma, and amputation to describe the terrain and the cataclysmic forces that they thought had created it.

It was a hiker, not a trained geologist, who first posited that the Sierra were gently sculpted over eons by the slow and persistent scouring of glaciers. I like the fact that a hiker figured it out—that you don't have to understand words like geomorphic, autobrecciated, or granodiorite pluton, to be able to read the landscape; that polysyllables don't have to meaninglessly ramble around your skull until your mind goes numb for you to understand that the moraine you have to climb over was put there by a glacier, and that the glacier also scoured the cirque above you. I like the fact that geology can be—although it seldom is—as clear as highcountry air.

So let us return to our astute hiker, armed with a pair of eyes and the curiosity to use them, and let's listen to what he has to say: "The Master Builder chose for a tool, not the earthquake nor lightning to rend asunder, not the stormy torrent nor eroding rain, but the tender snow-flowers, noiselessly falling through unnumbered seasons, the offspring of sun and sea."

Do you recognize the mixture of poetry and science? John Muir, of course. The year is 1874.

Enter the learned opposition, armed with impressive credentials and attitudes to match. Listen to Professor Josiah Dwight Whitney, head of the California State Geological Survey, as he clears his throat and declares that John Muir is "a mere sheepherder, an ignoramus," and, furthermore, "A more absurd theory was never advanced than that by which it was sought to ascribe to glaciers the sawing out of these vertical walls and the rounding of the domes. This theory, based on ignorance of the whole subject, may be dropped without wasting any more time upon it."

Clarence King, fabled Sierran explorer, author of the classic *Mountaineering in the Sierra Nevada*, and member of the California State Geological Survey, adds his two cents: Muir's theory, says he, is hogwash. There are no glaciers in the Sierra. He finishes with withering dismissal. "It is to be hoped that the ambitious amateur may divert his evident enthusiastic love of nature into a channel, if there is one, in which his attainments would save him from hopeless floundering."

Credentialed and learned they may be; they are also dead wrong.

The details can be (and are being) argued, but today it is generally accepted that the mountains we call the Sierra Nevada began to rise from the bed of their ancestral sea some 60 million years ago. Plate collision was the precipitating force, but (Messrs. Whitney and King notwithstanding) the Sierra were raised not by a single violent event, but rather by a series of collisions that took place over a period of some 20 million years.

Then, about 2.5 million years ago, came the ice. At the height of North America's glaciation, 20,000–60,000 years ago, the Sierra was covered with a frozen sheet perhaps 100 miles long, 60 miles wide, and 4,000 feet deep. The glaciers advanced, cutting into the rock and earth, then retreated, dragging

KAREN FORDING WHITNEY CREEK

their rubble with them. Like water, they took the easiest path downhill, cutting through what could be cut, carving what could be carved, polishing the rest.

Nowhere is the glaciation more evident than in the High Sierra. Here is the rocky heart, the *sanctum sanctorum* of these great mountains, the landscape made sacred by John Muir and Ansel Adams. Starting at Cottonwood Pass and running to the northern part of Yosemite, the High Sierra is characterized by elevations from 8,000 to more than 14,000 feet, and by evidence of glaciation, including scoured cirques, lateral and terminal moraines, and countless lakes and tarns.

At Cottonwood Pass, elevation 11,160 feet, I feel the high thin air biting into my lungs for the first time, feel my legs telling my lungs, "Work harder, work harder." For the next 100 miles we will drop below 8,000 feet only three times; more commonly, the trail will stay above 10,000 feet.

Experienced mountaineers would scoff at these elevations, but they are high enough to cause some physiological changes in humans. Our blood thickens; thus it becomes more important to drink water frequently. Our pulse rises and our breathing becomes more labored than usual. Lack of oxygen can lead to headaches and nausea—as well as more serious effects such as pulmonary and cerebral edemas. Indeed, in the contiguous United States, the average elevation at which hikers and climbers suffer potentially fatal edemas is only 12,000 feet. Fortunately, acute mountain sickness (also called altitude sickness) is easily avoided if you take the time to acclimate. Thru-hikers aren't so much at risk because we've been climbing up and down mountains for weeks, and—most important—our approach to the higher elevations is slow and gentle. Still, most of us are at least a little short of breath.

Four days after leaving Kennedy Meadows, we reach Whitney Creek, which drains the west side of Mount Whitney. From our campsite the mountain is not visible. The valley is surrounded with strident, dramatic peaks, each taller and more imposing than the last. If mountains could talk, every one of them would be clamoring, "Over here! I'm the big one! Hey you, climb this way." And sure enough, just about every hiker gazes at one or another of the show-offy pinnacles and declares himself Whitney-bound.

There's a long tradition here of summiting the wrong peak. Remember Clarence King? The last time we met him, he was insulting John Muir. Let's rejoin him now, and watch his comeuppance at the hands of Mount Whitney.

In 1871, King set out to be the first person to stand atop the highest peak in the Sierra Nevada. He duly completed his climb and declared himself successful. But in 1873, the California Academy of Sciences, having studied the matter, declared that he had not been on the highest peak at all; he had mistakenly climbed a lesser mountain. King hurried back to the Sierra, still hoping to make the first ascent. Alas, when he finally reached the summit of the true high point, he found a cairn and a note announcing the presence of two previous parties.

Down below, yet another brouhaha was underway. Earlier in the summer, three fishermen had climbed into the mountains to escape the heat of the Owens Valley and had decided to do a little peak bagging. Up they went, until there was nothing left between them and the sky. When they returned, they announced their achievement and the mountain they had climbed became locally known as Fishermen's Peak. But although their claim was upheld (theirs was the real first ascent, and they had left evidence on the summit), the name Fishermen's Peak was not to be. Since the earliest days of Sierran exploration, the members of various surveys had intended to name the highest peak after Josiah Dwight Whitney, chief of the California State Geological Survey. The fact that for some years the name had been attached to the wrong peak was neither here nor there. Now that the identity of the highest peak was established, the name and the mountain could finally be reconciled.

Shortly afterward, John Muir attempted to climb to the summit—and also found himself on the wrong peak. Unlike King, he realized his error immediately, went back down, resupplied, turned around, and headed straight up again.

Nowadays, the climb to Whitney's summit is one of the most popular hikes in the Sierra, and it requires a permit which can be difficult to get. Dan and I both have the necessary stamp on our thru-hikers

East Vidette Mountain and Bubbs Creek basin, Kings Canyon National Park

permit, but I'm not climbing. I've been up Whitney a couple of times before, and with my bad foot, I've decided that my thru-hiking aspirations are better served by forward motion and rest than by pretending to be a mountain goat.

So while Dan rises at five to climb alone, I luxuriate in camp. I sleep in until the unheard of hour of nine o'clock, and then turn to chores: sorting food and washing clothes in water so cold my hands cramp. I fill a dark water bag from the stream and set it in the sun to warm so Dan can have a not-quite ice-cold shower when he comes down from the mountain. And then I snuggle into my sleeping bag and spend the day reading Muir.

"Well-seasoned limbs will easily enjoy the climb of 9,000 feet required for this direct route, but soft, succulent people should go the mule way," he writes. The direct route is up the eastern slope. (Just to put things in perspective, let me say that never, no matter how physically fit I have been—and that includes a triathlon and two marathons—have I easily enjoyed any climb of 9,000 feet.) The "mule way," in case you're wondering, is the climb from the western side, where we are camped. It merely requires a 16-mile round trip and 4,000 feet of elevation gain.

Muir is rhapsodically in his element:

> *We rose early and were off in the first flush of dawn . . . passing . . . along the north shore of a glacier lake whose simple newborn beauty enhanced us all . . . Along its northern shore we sped joyously, inspired with the fresh unfurling beauties of the morning . . . every muscle in harmonious accord . . . Above the second lake basin we found a long upcurving field of frozen snow, across which we scampered, with our breasts filled with exhilarating azure, leaping with excess of strength . . . Higher and higher we climbed with muscles in excellent poise, the landscape becoming more and more glorious as the wild alps rose in the tranquil sky.*

When Dan returns to the meadow where I am camped, he looks exactly like someone who has spent the day scampering about with an excess of strength and a breast filled with exhilarating azure. He suggests that we pack up camp and hike on another five miles. The reason is not only an abundance of energy. The unreliable but compelling rumor mill has it that Wallace Creek, five miles away, is running high. The flow of these snowmelt-fed streams fluctuates with the time of day. If we continue on and camp by the stream tonight, we can cross it first thing in the morning when its flow will be slower, because the snowfields that feed it melt less rapidly during the cold alpine nights. I'm happy to hike on; after all, I've been sitting around all day reading John Muir, who describes one of the river crossings up ahead in florid detail:

> *The descent of the Kings River streams is mostly made in the form of cascades . . . (some of which) . . . are squeezed in narrow-throated gorges, boiling, seething, in deep swirling pools, . . . breaking into ragged, tossing masses of spray and foam in boulder-choked canyons . . . giving forth a great variety of wild mountain melody, which, rolling from side to side against the echoing cliffs, is at length all combined into one smooth, massy, sea-like roar.*

June 21. Day 47. Mile 764. Wallace Creek.

My fourth climb of Whitney but the first time solo in snow. After a predawn start, I reached the summit at about nine o'clock. In mid-summer, I've sometimes seen more than 100 people struggling to get up here like an army of ants. But this morning, I was the sole person atop the mountain. Walking alone through the needle-like gendarmes that guard the summit ridge, I was the highest person in the contiguous United States. The climb was not nearly as difficult as I had expected, which I'm taking as good news as far as the passes ahead are concerned. After finishing the climb, I rested in camp for a couple of hours, and then we decided to go on. I'm glad we did, because the creek is indeed running high. Hopefully, the flow will be slower by morning.

—Dan's journal

Shooting star in Glen Pass, Kings Canyon National Park

Lower Palisades Lake, Kings Canyon National Park

Moonrise over Wanda Lake, Kings Canyon National Park

Sunset over McGee Lakes basin, Kings Canyon National Park

The roar of the creek keeps me awake, even though I'm an especially talented sleeper. On a hiking trip I can easily sleep for 10 hours; on a winter backpacking trip, I'm good for 12. But tonight, I keep listening for the creek to subside. I know this is irrational; it's not like the creek will be roaring one moment and whispering the next. But I keep listening anyway. The decibel level stays constant. If the snowfields are melting up top, it hasn't yet affected the flow down here.

And then, I hear another sound that makes me forget all about the roaring creek.

A snort, followed by lumbering footsteps, followed by a metallic clank.

"Oh, crap," Dan says, because he knows exactly what it is, and so do I.

A bear.

A bear of an ordinarily unprepossessing species: *Ursus Americanus* (that part means black bear), but a fearsome subspecies: *national parkus pestus*.

Black bears are usually shy. In my hiking career, I've seen more of them than I can remember, and most of them have exhibited the same response: they flee. Most of my black bear photographs, therefore, are more accurately described as pictures of black bear butts taken while the bear is making haste for somewhere else. Since bears are bigger than me, and have big claws and big teeth, I appreciate this standoffishness.

But the national park subspecies is altogether a different creature, an ursine outlaw that has learned its thieving ways at its mother's knee. Nowhere are these pests more feared than in Kings Canyon, Sequoia, and Yosemite National Parks. Blame it on the fact that park bears are not hunted, hence develop no fear of humans. Blame it on the number of park visitors, which increases bear/human interactions. Blame it on the rangers, who relocate especially troublesome bears to the backcountry so they can prey on hikers' food sacks rather than car-campers' coolers. Blame it on human stupidity; bears show far more intelligence and resourcefulness at getting food from people than people do at keeping bears away from food.

Sometime in the last 30 years, park bears figured out that humans carry food, and that this food tastes a lot better than the grubs and worms and seeds that your basic normal bear considers bear food. For *Ursus Americanus national parkus pestus*, summer is spent in the nonstop pursuit of macaroni and cheese, trail mix, Snickers bars, and oatmeal.

You cannot hike the Sierra without hearing a bear story. Trail lore says that bears walk around at night sniffing tree branches to locate food. (Bear bagging, as it's called, is the traditional technique for putting food out of harm's way by hanging it from a tree branch.) When the bear locates the food, it climbs the tree, crawls out on the branch, and tears the rope so the food falls down. Supposedly, if the tree branch from which the food sacks hang is too thin to hold the weight of an adult, mama bear will send her babies out to retrieve the food sack.

If you think these are hiker tall tales, all you have to do is look at the spider's web of broken rope that hangs from the tree branches around any well-used campsite.

Our food is stored in a bear box, a metal bear-proof food locker installed by the Park Service at some—but not enough—of the popular campsites. (Hence the metal clanking.) I guess you could argue (and I'm sure someone has argued) that the bear boxes are contrary to the spirit of wilderness. But they seem a good idea to me: if bears figured out that they couldn't get people food, they'd go back to eating bear food—if, at this point, they even remember what that is.

The national parks also sell and rent supposedly bear-proof food sacks, which weigh about 3 pounds and can hold about a 5-day supply of food. For us, that's not a feasible solution: with a 15-day supply of food, each of us would need three of them, which would add an extra 9 pounds to each of our packs, if we could fit the containers inside, which I doubt. So whenever we can, we camp at sites that have bear-proof storage lockers; when that isn't possible, we hang our food and make a burglar alarm by piling ice axes and walking sticks around the tree trunks. The idea is that when the bear climbs the tree, he'll knock over the metal axes and sticks, which will make noise and scare him away—or at least wake us up so we can throw rocks at him.

Rain drenched Trail, Kings Canyon National Park

Marie Lake, John Muir Wilderness

This particular bear is small as bears go, and our food, being safely ensconced in the box, isn't in any danger. But I have to admit that at three o'clock in the morning when you're sleeping in a nylon tent, no bear that is rummaging around your campsite only a few yards away is going to really seem small. By morning, I am more than happy to get up and face the creek.

The last time Dan and I crossed Wallace Creek, it was a meek-looking August trickle and, as I recall, a string of llamas was fording it alongside of us. I think I rock-hopped across without even getting my feet wet. Now, that meek-looking trickle is a frothing torrent barely contained by its braided gravel channels.

The flow this morning is somewhat slower than it was last night, but at a cost: the freezing nighttime temperatures have very nearly managed to turn the water back to ice.

Numbness starts creeping up one leg before I've even got the other in the water. My instinct is to bolt across like a racehorse, but the streambed is rocky, and in the crashing white water I can't see where I'm stepping. Instead, I have to feel for the footing even as my feet are losing feeling. The water is fast, and thigh deep; the sound is a low roar.

The key here is concentration. I cannot think about the other bank, or how far away it still is. I have to block out the roar, forget about finishing, and think only of the next slow, deliberate step.

You know how sometimes when you go to the dentist, the novocaine wears off before the pain does? When I reach the far bank and climb out of the almost-frozen water, feeling returns with a vengeance, as if a thousand knives were severing the nerves in my legs.

Still, the salient fact is this: Dan and I have both reached the other side of the first big creek. He, in addition, has climbed Whitney. Which means that we have come face to face with the evil twins of the Sierran snowmelt: the highcountry ice-pack and the valley fords. There is plenty more of each ahead, but when we walk on from Wallace Creek, there is just the slightest hint of a swagger in our stride.

A few miles later at Tyndall Creek, we come upon our old pal, Steve, who is sitting on a rock looking as pleased with himself as we feel.

"Hey! Whatcha doing up so high?" he calls out.

"We got lost on our way to the sky," I say.

He is bursting with excitement. He has just, he tells us, climbed Forester Pass in the moonlight.

Or so he thinks. Forester Pass is the first of the big passes. It is, however, still 5 miles away. The pass Steve thought he had climbed was really a plateau; in the dark, he had matched the guidebook's landmarks—lakes and streams and such—with the wrong features. Considering how different the two places actually are, it's a funny mistake to have made, except, I suppose, if you're the one who made it. Imagine thinking you've crossed the 20-mile mark in a marathon only to learn that no, it was really just milepost 13. Steve is first incredulous, then shrugs his shoulders and says, "Oh, well."

Now, the high passes lie just ahead: Forester Pass, 13,200; Glen Pass, 11,978; Pinchot Pass, 12,130; Mather Pass, 12,100; Muir Pass, 11,955; Selden Pass, 10,900; Silver Pass, 10,900; Donohue Pass, 11,056.

I am ready for these numbers, ready for the dizzying heights, the lung-scouring air, the snow underfoot. I am ready to walk on rocks that are broken chunks of the same craggy granite that pokes up to the sky.

"Away we go to the topmost mountains," says Muir. "Many still small voices as well as the noon thunder are calling, come higher."

So we do.

Forester Pass is a gun-sight sized notch in a 1,000-foot rock wall. The approach is innocuous enough—a long gentle climb up a valley. The trail is alternately snow covered and waterlogged but the route is clear: it goes to the wall that looms ahead, seemingly impenetrable. And you wonder: Where could someone have put a trail? You hope that perhaps there is a cut in the cliff that you can't see. Or that the trail circles around to some hidden lower notch. Because they simply can't intend for you to go up and over *that*.

But, no. Your path leads you on, and up, and the wall is still as stark and steep as a fortress.

Even in mid-summer, when there is no snow, the thin gray trail is hard to see; it seemingly vanishes into its gray granite background. Now, in June, there is another problem: the base of the pass is under snow. You have to look higher, where the wall steepens and the snow can't cling, before you see the occasional fragment of a path.

When you do see it, you might wish you didn't. The only way to get to the trail is to climb straight up through the snow. Then the path heads across an ice slope underneath a cornice that looks like it has the fairly immediate intention of plummeting into the valley below.

It does not look like it can be done.

But it can. At least 50 people left Kennedy Meadows before us. There is no stack of bodies at the bottom of the pass, nor have we seen a parade of defeated hikers who turned back. Somehow, they got up and over. Which means that we can, too.

It makes me understand in a way I never have the difference between the first person to do something and everybody else. It is the confirmation of the possible.

The climb is shorter than we expect. The cornice is scary but apparently solid, and there's a nice wide shelf to step onto. From there, it's only a matter of seconds until we are up at the windy notch that marks the boundary between Sequoia and Kings Canyon national parks, where the known world doubles.

Previously, the northern sky was filled by the wall of the pass. Now it is filled with a sea of snow-capped mountains extending into infinity. Below us, a wintry blanket of snowfields covers the cold northern slope. It is desolate, magnificent, stark, sublime. This is eye-popping, jaw-dropping country. I could camp up here for a week and not be able to comprehend it all. What I do comprehend is that in order to be here and see this, you must walk where we have walked and climb what we have climbed. There is no other way.

Wrote Muir:

> *The scenery of all the passes, especially at the head, is of the wildest and grandest description—lofty peaks massed together and laden around their bases with ice and snow, chains of glacier lakes, cascading streams in endless variety, with glorious views . . . Every pass, however, possesses treasures of beauty all its own and the finding of these is one of the mountaineer's exceedingly great rewards.*

We can see our route north from here. It plummets to the valley below, then rises right back up again into those mountains ahead that cling to the sky. Our fate, thus laid out clearly before us, seems so obviously simple. So simply impossible.

But it isn't: there are half-frozen, sun-softened footsteps in the snow. Again, they confirm the possible. What, I wonder, would it be like to be the first hiker of the season?

Forester Pass, it turns out, is not the most difficult pass, although comparisons are hard to make. Not only does each pass possess its own treasures of beauty, it also offers its own unique variation on the theme of highcountry snow travel. Also, each hiker has his or her own idea of what is hard and what is easy.

There are four of us now: Tom caught us last night. We're glad for the convivial company, plus there is safety in numbers.

At Glen Pass, the theme is hide and seek. As soon as we reach the snow line, the trail develops an irritating habit of slipping under a snow patch and then veering off in a different direction. Once, it actually heads underwater, to a signed junction located in the middle of an seasonal snowmelt lake.

Devils Postpile, Devils Postpile National Monument

57

Banner Peak reflected in unnamed lake, Ansel Adams Wilderness

But when we can take a moment to stop looking for the trail and instead look at the fierce beauty around us, there's no dissent: it's worth every bit of effort to be here. Approaching Glen Pass, the trail takes us past a tarn surrounded by a gigantic amphitheater of rock and snow. The water is a palette of blues and greens the color of jewels: jade, lapis lazuli, and shining sapphires speckled with diamond glints of sunlight. Where a pool of mineral-tinted water lies atop a submerged iceberg, the water is turquoise or emerald, depending on the depth of the water and the position of the sun. In the deep cold shade of an overhanging cliff, the water is black like onyx, and still as a mirror.

Now, the trail turns ornery. The slopes are steep and if you fall, chances are good that you will end up somewhere you really don't want to be. The trick, of course, is not to fall. We overtake a group of hikers who are having trouble in that regard. Only out for a five-day hike, they didn't bring ice axes or even walking sticks, and they are flailing about in a way that would be hilarious if wasn't horrifying. It's not like we're having such an easy time ourselves: with each step, the snow and scree underfoot seem intent on sliding down the mountain. Up the down escalator we go.

And we get there. A few minutes later, we're joined by two of the ice axe-less hikers, on the adrenaline high you get when you climb something big and hard. The others have turned back. The two who made it are in a celebratory frame of mind; they're not thinking about the downside—the literal, physical downside—of the pass.

The downslide.

Dan and I tackle it first, following a path of sun-softened footsteps. This is an act of faith, since the angle of the slope prevents us from seeing where the steps actually go. They go across the slope and a little way down. And then they stop. Looking down, we see swath-like paths—butt-prints.

At some point, it is easier to let gravity have its way. Dan and I sit, and, one at a time, we push off downhill, holding our ice axes behind us like rudders. The idea is that if we get going too fast, we can use the axe as a brake. If we careen out of control, we can simply pivot toward the slope and dig the pick of the axe into the snow. On the way downhill, I do this several times for practice, just to remind myself that it does indeed work.

At the bottom of the slope we look back up and see the axe-less hikers laboriously kicking in steps and climbing down backwards, one step at a time, face-to-snowfield. I don't think I have ever witnessed something so terrifying.

But we have our own problems.

Below us are Rae Lakes. I'm sure it would not be exaggerating to call this alpine basin one of the most stupendously beautiful in the world. Each time I have been here, this view of lakes and mountains has made me gasp. The water in the two large lakes is a dark somber green, but it is also crystal clear. You can see logs on the bottom of the lake, and rocks, and fish (unfortunately, none of them big enough to eat).

The water is very deep. Our guidebook laconically warns us that in early season, the crossing of the outlet stream between the lakes can be wet.

By "wet" the authors must mean that if we tried to wade across we would be dog paddling in water up to our eyeballs.

Bridging the outlet is a thrown-together collection of logs that look slippery as ice and precarious as a surfboard. When I tentatively place one foot on one of them, it starts to roll. The others are slightly more stable, but in essence, I am going to be trying to cross the outlet on a floating, rolling balance beam covered with algae. The crossing takes about half an hour because that's how long Dan and I spend staring at the logs in disbelief.

It seems that we are spending a lot of time these days staring at obstacles in disbelief. I have first-hand evidence that my adrenaline-producing glands are working just fine.

By now the pattern is predictable: up all morning, down all afternoon. The progress is either slow or it is slower. The day we climbed Forester, we covered 14.1 miles; the day we climbed Glen, we covered 16.3 miles. The next pass is Pinchot. From our camp at Woods Creek, it is 7.1 miles to the pass. It takes us seven hours to get there.

A THRU-HIKER COUNTS AND SORTS FOOD FOR THE LONG STRETCH OF TRAIL AHEAD

This is not due to any particular difficulty of Pinchot Pass. Indeed, technically, Pinchot is probably the easiest of the high passes.

But picture that you are walking up a valley, gently ascending toward a pronounced and conspicuous pass. Your train of thought might go something like this:

We must climb up and over a pass.

There is a pass ahead of us.

The trail we are hiking on is going directly toward that pass.

Therefore, we are supposed to climb that pass.

Dan and I remember camping here on our honeymoon. (I threw a rope in the air to hang our food in a tree, and hit him in the face with a carabiner.) We even remember exchanging comments that there was something funky about where the route went; that it might be tricky in snow if you weren't paying attention.

And still, we find ourselves at the head of the valley, looking for a trail to the wrong pass. Fortunately, my compass isn't prone to making obvious but incorrect assumptions. It insists that if we are standing where we think we are standing, we are not going where we think we are going. It takes awhile before we get the map and the compass and the terrain and our minds all lined up facing the right direction. Pinchot Pass, sneaky thing, is lurking off to the left.

June 24. Day 50. Mile 808. South Fork Kings River.

The stream crossings made today the toughest to date.

Atop a high pass, all is white and quiet. As you descend, you hear little dripping trickles. Soon, there are freshets to step over. Then streams. Then you have to rock-hop, then ford. The fords deepen: at the outlet creek of Lake Marjorie, the water was waist-deep.

Soon after we dropped into treeline, I heard a distant roar, and the only thing it could be was the South Fork of the Kings River, far below. As we continued the seemingly endless descent, we could see all the waterfalls and cascades coming down from the snow-covered heights. All that water was headed into the river below—the river that we had to cross. More and more water kept falling, and the roar got louder and louder so that by the time I finally actually saw it, I was relieved that the river was merely a foaming, fast-moving white-water torrent pouring over car-sized boulders and not something worse—like Niagara Falls. We had to cross it tonight rather than in the morning because there was nowhere to camp on the near side. Karen scouted a route, but when the three of us reached her proposed crossing, we unanimously agreed that she had lost her mind. But a crossing it was, of sorts. As I fought my way across a streambed filled with boulders that I couldn't see under the fast-moving, churning, waist-deep water, I tried not to think about what would happen if I fell or was swept over by the current. It didn't even matter that my pack took in water. I think I have never been as glad to be back on terra firma. I cannot help but think that tomorrow we'll probably have to do this—or something just like it—all over again.

—DAN'S JOURNAL

From the valley, Mather Pass looks like it's going to give us a break. The vertical distance from base to summit is a mere 500 feet. I remember the pass as an easy one, although I am beginning to realize that my memory is more like a sieve than a steel trap.

The problem Mather presents is straightforward: except for a single switchback way to the right of the pass, the entire trail is under snow. At Forester and Glen—even at Pinchot—we could cobble together patches of existing trail, but here it's pointless to guess where the trail might go: for us, the only way is a straight-up assault.

Deer along the shore of Thousand Island Lake, Ansel Adams Wilderness

Thousand Island Lake in evening light, Ansel Adams Wilderness

Not being one of those conquer-the-mountains types, I use the word assault advisedly. Sitting atop an alpine summit, I have often felt like a laborer, a supplicant, a celebrant, an adventurer, a daredevil, an achiever, a meditator, and the luckiest person alive, but I have never felt like much of a conqueror. That relationship is not in my nature and I don't think it's much in the nature of mountains, either.

Likewise, I don't tend to think of climbing as an assault. It seems logical that something you assault can assault you right back. Speaking strictly for myself, I don't have any illusions about who—me or the mountain—would come out the worse for wear.

But for some reason, the ascent up Mather Pass seems an assault. Perhaps I am not fighting the mountain, but my own fear.

It is by doing things like this that I have learned that I am afraid of heights. Phobias, of course, deal in perceptions, not reality. I don't have to be atop a dangerous icy pass to be all sweaty-palmed and shaky; I can get that way on a perfectly good fire tower with handrails. In this case, the danger is both real and imagined.

Our route takes us the direct way, straight up the left side. As long as my face is pretty much pressed up against the wall of a snowbank on this steep ascent, I don't have to see the ice-clotted lake at the base of the pass, which is where I will end up if I fall. It's only when I can see the empty space below that my mouth goes dry, my stomach churns, and all the blood in my body seems to be pounding somewhere behind my ears.

Plant the ice-axe, kick a step, check your balance, repeat the process. Don't look down, don't look down, don't look down.

Strangely, I don't mind doing this. In a weird way, I'm enjoying my fear. This kind of hiking is intensely present-tense. There's no room for daydreaming or—my other favorite pastime—for writing books in my head. Here, the immediate task demands concentration. Only this moment exists: there is no past, no future. Somewhere in the world I left behind, I have a family and friends and a house and a career. But just exactly now, that other world might as well be Mars. None of it has anything to do with me. My life is whittled down to the feel of my axe gripping the snow, the traction of my boots, my balance as I take the next step, plant boot to snow, test my footing, step again.

Forester Pass was straightforward, Glen was gnarly, Pinchot was the trickster, and Mather was frightening. Muir, the gentlest of the five passes we've climbed so far, is just simply long.

You might think gentle equates with easy, but the gain of elevation from the Middle Fork of the Kings River to Muir Pass is 4,000 feet, so forget about easy.

But the major difficulty, again, is the snow. The other passes quickly vault over their high points and plummet back down, but the trail over Muir Pass climbs above the 10,000-foot snow line, then lingers there for about 10 miles, meandering from basin to basin. It is well into the afternoon before we are even close to the pass, and that means that the sun has softened the snow. Springtime alpine snow has the tendency to freeze overnight and melt during the day. As it melts, little irregularities in the snow create patterns called sun-cups, which look very much like egg cartons. As the day proceeds, the depressions grow deeper, making the surface difficult to walk on, and to make things even worse, the crust of the snow starts to soften so that with every step, we are subject to suddenly breaking through the surface and plunging thigh-deep into the snow. Slipping and sliding, we proceed higher, looking for a trail that was right underfoot a moment ago and has now disappeared, perhaps forever. Tom and Steve have disappeared, too: they got ahead of us and must have chosen a different path; their footsteps are nowhere to be found.

We continue up, past still, frozen lakes, surrounded by rock and ice, snow and water, gray granite, cyan sky. There is not a hint of life, not a smidgen of green. A piercing whistle stops us in our tracks.

I figure it's Tom or Steve saying something like, "This way, stupid," but there is no sign of either of them, and still no footsteps.

Another whistle, and then an outraged, awkward scurrying that is the part waddle and part outright run of a yellow-bellied marmot, otherwise known as *Marmota flaviventris*.

Heading north along the Trail with Mount Ritter and Banner Peak in the background, Ansel Adams Wilderness

Deer grazing in Tuolumne Meadows, Yosemite National Park

Leconte Falls, Yosemite National Park

Down among the trees, you'd hardly notice the little fella. Marmots are the largest members of the ground squirrel family, also the largest true hibernators, but at 14–18 inches long, they're only about the size of an opossum or a small raccoon.

I have an affinity for marmots; they have exquisite taste in living quarters. Preferring the highcountry above the lodgepole belt, they are found most often above treeline, in rocky outcroppings near meadows. Their homes are in exactly the kind of terrain I like the best. And one more thing: they refuse to be kept in captivity.

Finally, we invade the marmot's sense of personal space and it scurries off, squeezing its plump little body into what seems like an impossibly small crevasse.

Muir Pass is different from all the others: there's a hut at the top, made of rocks from the mountain. In mid-summer, it blends in so well with its surroundings that you might not even see it at first. Just at the moment, the ground is covered in snow and the cabin is immediately visible. Tom and Steve are waiting for us inside. Jason is there, too; he's one of the hikers we met early on in the trip, and we've been crossing paths with him fairly regularly since.

I sink onto one of the benches and wonder how I'm going to find the strength to get up and go on. I am completely exhausted. I don't even manage to summon up enough energy to sign the hiker register.

Much as I might like to stay here indefinitely, we can't. First of all, it's illegal; the hut is an emergency shelter only. And second, while the hut would doubtless be a lifesaver in a storm, it gives new meaning to the term stone-cold. Afternoon is wearing away, the snow is getting softer and softer. After only a 10-minute rest, I give up my perch and reluctantly start post-holing down the other side of the pass. My heel doesn't much appreciate the jolt it feels each time I break through the sun-cups. My pace slows to a crawl as I try to find a line of travel that won't have me sinking up to my thighs every time I take a step. Finally, Dan suggests that we just pitch our tent any old place. Except we can't: everywhere we look, the ground is either too rocky or waterlogged.

Finally, we find a spot exactly big enough for our tent, and not an inch bigger. Tom and Steve continue on; they are determined not to spend the night camped on snow. Dan and I squeeze into our little site, jammed between a snowbank and Wanda Lake, elevation 11,400 feet.

Here, in our highest campsite, winter has not completely abdicated its reign over a frosty kingdom. The wind blows cold breath across the ice-clotted lake. Our world comprises granite, snow, a lake, and a sky that cannot decide what color it wants to be. Over the course of an hour, it tries on different cloaks: bright blue, then orange and pink, followed by a dusky purple; finally it settles on black, star-studded with sequins. The wind dies down and silence descends, broken only by the gentle lapping of the lake against its rocky shore. Sometimes the crash of a falling rock punctures the quiet.

In the morning, the lake is covered with a thin coat of ice. The lids to our water bottles are frozen shut, so we stick them in our armpits to warm them. I have to break through the lake's coat of ice by banging my cookpot against it in order to get water for breakfast. Our boots, soaked from yesterday's post-holing, are also frozen. We pour boiling water into our water bottles and put the bottles inside the boots. This isn't a comfy-cozy, warm-the-tootsies thing; without being warmed, the frozen boots are too stiff to put on our feet.

But when we finally get going and descend out of the snow into the steep-walled canyon of the Evolution Valley, the hard work is finished, at least for now. Before us are still three more passes. But all of them are about 1,000 feet lower than the five passes we have just crossed. It is also a few days later in the season, days during which snow has been melting. What lies ahead will not be as difficult as what lies behind.

SWITCHBACKS ON THE GOLDEN STAIRCASE

June 27. Day 53. Mile 848. Piute Pass Trail Junction.

If it feels like we're beginning to fly, there's a reason for it. Not only have we crossed the mighty passes; we're traveling lighter. Our obese packs have slimmed down, and given our diets, I'd be surprised if we haven't dropped a few pounds, too. Most of the thru-hikers we've seen seem to be feeling equal parts exhilaration and exhaustion. Today just after we crossed Evolution Creek, a hiker named Nester caught us. He's an Asian-American cable-car operator from San Diego, who we met for the first time just south of Kennedy Meadows. Crossing Evolution Creek, he made the mistake of going dead center through the deepest part and got knocked off his feet by the current. There was a dramatic pause before he found his feet again and scrambled over to our side of the creek.

He told us that he had hiked the entire Sierra alone, which he obviously found difficult. I can imagine why: not only are you in danger of falling down a mountain slope, but traveling solo, you're in danger of no one knowing you're there. He greeted us with a heartfelt, "I'm so glad to see some other hikers!" When we left the creek, he was still drying out his waterlogged gear, but he showed up tonight in our camp and is going to walk with us tomorrow. I think he's glad to have someone to talk to.

—DAN'S JOURNAL

In a way it's funny that we're so isolated. From my previous visits to the Sierra, I remember Evolution Valley as jam-packed with hikers, with tents on every little flat spot, and lots of large groups. Later in the season, you might see 100 or more people marching over the passes: scout troops, Sierra Clubbers, church groups, you name it.

There's no doubt that I'd rather brave the snowy passes if I can have the solitude that comes with hiking off-season. With few exceptions, the High Sierra is populated only with long-distance hikers in June, and there aren't many of us. One of those exceptions is the area around Vermillion Valley, which is lower in elevation (hence no snow) and close to a road (hence, you don't have to walk far to get here.)

Nester has a resupply at Vermillion Valley, so we part company. As I watch him heading off for a shower and a meal, I'm second-guessing our decision not to stop there. After 13 days, I could use a break, and the thru-hikers we see returning from their rest stop seem to think it was well worth the detour. But our Reds Meadow resupply is just two days ahead.

I've often found that the smaller units of the national park system have a friendlier feel than the larger, more famous parks. Rangers are more likely to compare notes about their favorite campsite than they are to check your permits, the campgrounds are smaller and quieter, and there are fewer so-called amenities of the stuffed-animal and key-chain variety. Devil's Postpile National Monument, along with adjacent Reds Meadow, features a rock formation of a columnar lava flow with a glacially polished top; it looks like a 300-foot-long, 200-foot-high pile of petrified fence posts. This early in the season, the park is very quiet and unpopulated.

Reds Meadow—the resupply toward which we have been walking for 200 miles—seems like Mecca, although it comprises only a little general store, a cafe, some cabins, and a campground where there is a shower-house fed hot water from a natural hot spring. The closer your stall is to the springs, the hotter the water. Dan and I choose the two closest stalls and I don't think I've ever had a shower that felt better.

We stay just long enough to resupply, get clean, eat two breakfasts apiece in the cafe, and trade notes with some fellow hikers. It would not be exaggerating to say that the overall feeling is just the slightest bit triumphant. When, two days later, we arrive in Tuolumne Meadows in Yosemite National Park, friends meet us and whisk us away to Mammoth Lakes for three days of R and R. There is no doubt that we have earned every second of it.

Tuolumne River, Yosemite National Park

Lake Harriet, Emigrant Wilderness

View north over Sonora Pass, Toiyabe National Forest

chapter 3

NORTHERN CALIFORNIA: HITTING THE WALL

Along with the physical hurdles—along with the passes, the rivers, the elephantine loads of food (and before that in the desert, the even more elephantine loads of water), along with all of that—somewhere, very recently, we have crossed an invisible hurdle.

By this point, fully one-third of the prospective thru-hikers have left the trail. At the Tuolumne Meadows Campground, hikers in casts and bandages (or needing them) are gathering belongings and making travel arrangements, having succumbed to strains and sprains and stress fractures and sore muscles, and some of them sore spirits, too. It is not easy to quit when you have come this far.

But we are among the survivors. Thru-hikers, for real.

It feels like we've been hiking forever.

And, let it be said, we're feeling a little chipper. The tough stuff is done; over; finito. There are no more dangerous ice slopes to cross, no more 12,000 foot passes to climb. We are leaving Tuolumne Meadows with five days of food, not 15.

In his 1946 book, *Pacific Crest Trails* (which proposed a route from—get this—Mount Katmai in Alaska to Cape Horn at the tip of South America), mountaineering enthusiast Joseph T. Hazard evaluated various trails to be included in the fledgling project. One of them was the Yosemite/Tahoe Trail, which we will follow off and on for about 100 miles.

"It is a dependable granite land with rock lakes, flower meadows, primitive forest," writes Hazard. "Its very lack of extremes makes it ideal packhorse or backpacker country with convenient and sheltered campsites. Summer weather is cool, water pure and fairly plentiful, fishing most inviting. Passes are easy, streams fordable, gorges kindly."

Well, glory be! We're ready for a few kindly gorges, for some easy passes, and for convenient, sheltered campsites.

There is one sour little note in this litany of optimism. Our guidebook warns us that over the next 75 miles, we'll sometimes feel that we're doing "more vertical climbing than horizontal walking."

Having come over the entire High Sierra in snowmelt, I refuse to worry. I've hiked northern Yosemite before, and I don't remember anything noteworthy in the vertical department. So I wave the words away like an irritating mosquito buzzing too close to my ear.

Oh, yes, one more thing: something about mosquitoes. William Brewer, one of Josiah Whitney's assistants, wrote, "Tuolomne was picturesque, romantic…but prosy truth bids me to say that mosquitoes swarmed in myriads."

Well, prosy truth bids me to say a few things, too.

I have often heard hikers on the Appalachian Trail muse about whether the mosquito that has been droning in their ear for the last hour is one mosquito buzzing along for the ride, or whether the mosquitoes work tag-team style, accompanying hikers through their home territory and then passing them off to the next bug in line.

Now I know. They are with you for the duration. Each of us has our own personal swarm that surrounds us like an aura. No matter where we go, there they are.

I do wonder how the mosquitoes ever get home again. Perhaps they trade off when two hikers traveling in the opposite directions meet and pass each other. I don't have a chance to learn the answer because we don't see too many other hikers. Those we do see have their shoulders to the grindstone and won't stop to talk. Neither will we. We can't. Mosquitoes love a stationary target. They invite their friends and relatives to come for dinner. They have mosquito banquets. They stay up and buzz all night, or until it gets too cold. Then, I don't know what they do: maybe they fall down in a drunk-on-blood stupor, or they fly crookedly home, crashing into trees. In any event, the next morning they are back again, a little sluggish, perhaps, but ready for work.

The few times we do take breaks, we look for cold, windy spots; preferably dry ones. At Bond Pass, we lunch in silent misery with five other hikers, all of us having chosen this spot in hopes of a breeze, a break, a brief respite from what seems like an unceasing and increasingly personal assault. Two hikers try to eat lunch while wearing head nets. One wears a full-body bug suit. Dan and I are wearing our Gore-Tex because the bugs can't bite through it. Nobody talks.

I don't know what's worse: climbs or stream fords. The temperature is in the high 80s, so going uphill in our Gore-Tex feels like running in a steam room, calisthenics in a sauna.

And just to set the record straight, the uphills are not at all the easy ascents I thought I recalled, but yes indeedy, vertical climbing, exactly as advertised.

The path is like the trajectory of a bouncing basketball, with an occasional slam-dunk thrown in for fun. The footway is poor, by which I mean rotten, crumbly, steep, and uneven. My heel aches with each step, especially when it lands on a rock that chooses that exact moment to abandon the spot where it has reposed for the last millennium in favor of a free fall to the valley floor. One day we walk for three hours to cover five miles. Downhill. I cannot believe that I could forget the difficulties of a hike like this until Dan reminds me that on our last trip we only covered about 10 miles a day—in August.

What a difference a month and more mileage can make! The increase in difficulty is exponential. In August, the Yosemite backcountry is everything a hiker could want. Climbs are easier when you don't have to sweat and swelter your way uphill wearing foul-weather gear as bug protection. The descents are gentler when the rocks are not slick with snowmelt.

(Since I can apparently no longer trust my memory about anything, I checked my diary of that 1993 Yosemite trip and found not one word of complaint, not even about mosquitoes. Instead, I found words like glorious and dramatic and stunning and breathtaking, along with descriptions of tight, steep, high-walled canyons, and granite mountain walls. I wish that I could summon up those rhapsodic reactions now that the going is tough, but I can't. I'm tough enough to endure, but not tough enough to enjoy.)

We cross the stream that feeds into Benson Lake, site of the so-called Benson Riviera, which, our guidebook assures us, every thru-hiker should and does visit. The snowmelt is in full swing now, and water has inundated the valleys. The stream fords are slow-moving and easy—certainly nothing like the High Sierra torrents—but they are also deep. Unless we want to walk in wet boots all day, we have to change into river sandals to cross.

This is a lot more tedious than you might think. One hand occupies itself with footwear while the other swats at the bugs that have figured out that hiker feet are DEET-free zones. Once you've crossed the stream, the whole process reverses.

Lichens, Emigrant Wilderness

And in the middle of all of this, our guidebook suggests that we walk over to this so-called Benson Riviera so that we can do what? Sunbathe! Swathed in Gore-Tex and bug repellent, Dan and I look at each other as though someone has suggested that we walk barefoot on coals.

Riviera or no Riviera, we are out of there as fast as we can put boots to feet and feet to trail. Our loyal swarms, of course, accompany us.

All this is the prosy truth.

For the first time since the very first day, the thought occurs to me: I don't have to do this. I have nothing to prove by making this journey. News flash, folks: *This is voluntary!* I don't much care for the idea of quitting, but I care less for misery. I'm out here to commune with nature, and nature is sticking its thumbs in its ears and wiggling its fingers at me.

I'm thinking woeful thoughts when, early in the morning of the second day, we run across a hiker traveling southbound—a thru-hiker: after some 900 miles on the trail, we recognize members of the tribe. The hiker coming toward us has a ratty old pack and muscles of steel and the far-sighted gaze of someone who's used to looking at distant vistas. But why is he going southbound? It's far too early in the season for anyone to have come down from Canada.

As it turns out, he's getting off the trail. (Note: Thru-hikers say someone "got off," which implies a reason, not that they "quit," which implies a weakness. We give each other the benefit of the doubt, knowing that we might need it ourselves sometime.) This particular hiker has developed nerve damage in his shoulder and arm, presumably from the weight of his pack. The pain is constant; he can barely move the arm. He's still second-guessing his decision, still coming to terms, trying to understand that—bam!—just like that, the hike is over. He provides the helpful information that up ahead there are places where the mosquitoes are pretty bad, places where they are really bad, and places where they are horrendous. And then, reluctantly, he heads back to Tuolumne Meadows and home.

Watching him go, I feel inexplicably, insanely lucky that my heel spur hasn't yet derailed my hike; that I will get to climb in the heat and wade through the streams and deal with my own personal swarm. Yippee!

So maybe it isn't yet time to quit, after all. It's not like there's any need to rush to a decision. I can quit anytime I like in the next 1,600 miles. Maybe all I needed was to give myself the option.

A day later, we hear a familiar greeting. "Hey! Whatcha doing up so high?"

It's our old pal Steve, who pulled ahead of us at Muir Pass. Steve resupplied at Vermillion Valley resort in the High Sierra, where he ate for three days straight in a vain attempt to gain weight. He says his energy level is low and he's worried about his health. He looks emaciated, and his clothes are hanging from his body like rags on a scarecrow. Steve confirms that Tom is several days ahead, having picked up his pace to something like 25 miles a day—or at least, that was his intent. I can't imagine what it would take for me to do 25 miles a day through this. More than I've got.

Steve agrees. "I'm thinking of slowing down," he says. "Have some fun, enjoy myself. Maybe come back and finish next year." He, too, has given himself permission to quit.

Which one of us will take himself or herself up on the offer?

If you're beginning to think that this doesn't sound like a lot of fun, you're right. There's too much sweat, too much work, a whole laundry list of niggling annoyances and major obstacles, not to mention those insufferable mosquitoes.

Whine, whine, whine.

Well okay, then, let's get down to brass tacks. Why do it, really?

In *Long-Distance Hiking: Lessons from the Appalachian Trail*, Roland Mueser conducted in-depth interviews of 136 thru-hikers. He concluded that people take to a long trail for three main reasons: A desire to live in the natural world, to escape or recuperate from some part of their lives back home, or for the physical challenge.

Lupine and Eagle Creek Dome, Mokelumne Wilderness

Lava flow, Mokelumne Wilderness

Lost Lake, Eldorado National Forest

Heather Lake, Desolation Wilderness

I think that for most hikers, all three factors are at work in some combination. Me, I lean to the communing-with-nature business (if not communing with mosquitoes), but I admit that there's a certain appeal in escaping some aspects of everyday life, especially the telephone. The physical challenge of long-distance hiking is not as compelling to me, perhaps because this is not my first long hike. It does, therefore, seem ironic that the PCT has been so heavy in the overcoming-adversity department.

In addition to those reasons, I propose another one: The chance to live entirely in the present tense; to slow down and experience very simple parts of life very intensely.

Dan adds another reason: The quest for the heroic. He points out that he will never catch the winning touchdown in the Superbowl, or even sit on the bench; ditto for hitting a home run in the World Series, running in the Olympics, or standing atop Mount Everest. But he can walk from Mexico to Canada. A long-distance hike is a chance for almost anybody to experience an epic adventure.

It's possible that we're over-intellectualizing something that is inbred. According to British writer Bruce Chatwin, long-distance walking is what comes naturally; it's the office and the automobile that we should be wondering about. Writes Chatwin:

> *In becoming human, man had acquired, together with his straight legs and striding walk, a migratory 'drive' or instinct to walk long distances through the seasons . . . This 'drive' was inseparable from his central nervous system . . . When warped in conditions of settlement, it found outlets in violence, greed, status-seeking, or mania for the new . . . The best thing is to walk. For life is a journey through wilderness.*

I believe him to be right about this. For me, there is a rightness and a balance to long-distance walking; its pace, its intensity, its simplicity.

But enough armchair philosophizing. All this makes for great discussion in a comfortable bar after the fact. But what about now, this minute, when the mosquitoes are biting and the trail is hard and no one—absolutely no one—is having even the slightest sliver of fun? Why not simply hitchhike around the problem, skip the tough stuff? Who cares if you walk 2,500 miles, not 2,600? No one will know.

Dan contends that it's a slippery slope: you compromise your hike once and the next thing you know, you've hitchhiked halfway to Canada.

I tend to agree. It seems to me that thru-hiking is an either/or proposition: Either you are thru-hiking or you are not.

All of us have to draw our lines in the sand. Having to skip a few days in the Mojave because of my injury is on one side of the line; bailing out of Yosemite because I can't cope with mosquitoes is way over on the other. Ray Jardine, whose *PCT Hiker's Handbook* can always generate a feisty debate among hikers, says something eminently sensible: "Shape your journey however you deem it will be most rewarding. And consider shaping it to resemble how you might wish to look back on it, years later."

Well, I would like to look back on myself as a cheerful hiking companion who rose to every occasion with a smile. I would like to remember myself as someone who whistled happy tunes while climbing steep, bug-infested mountains.

I guess everyone needs an impossible goal.

Nonetheless, a good goal it is. If I can't change nature, maybe I can change the way I approach it.

July 12. Day 67. Mile 1,013. Bridgeport motel.

Bridgeport is filled with hikers who look like they've just finished backpacking's version of the Burma death march. None of us expected to be here. Everyone is tired and behind schedule, shaking their heads in wonder that we have been beat to pieces, not by all those big-ticket dramas we worried about at the Mexican border, but by day-in day-out drudgery and annoyances.

One of the hikers said she spent most of the last few days crying in her tent, which made Karen, who spent most of the last few days in our tent complaining (although not crying), feel better. But Steve seems to have had the worst of it. Last we heard, he was headed off to a doctor. My guess is, we won't see him again on the trail.

—DAN'S JOURNAL

GROUSE HEN, DESOLATION WILDERNESS

At Sonora Pass, in one of those quicksilver changes that we should expect by now but seldom do, our universe simply changes.

I would love to chalk it up to successful attitude adjustment. But I can't—it wouldn't be prosy truth.

The change has nothing to do with attitude or taking a break in town or overcoming obstacles. It is simply the result of an entirely new geology.

Heretofore the mountains we have been walking over have been mostly granitic. That is, they are made up of rock that was originally liquid magma, but solidified while still beneath the earth's surface. Having been forged in extreme conditions over a long period of time, granitic rock (of which granite is only one kind) is extremely durable. It is also extremely resistant to glaciation except when it is jointed—which means that for some reason (let's leave it at that) the molecular bonds of the rock are subject to being cracked or broken. Glaciers slide over unjointed surfaces smoothly, with little to stop their flow. But when they encounter joints, they get purchase and cut and scour things, like the basins of all those jewel-colored tarns that dot the High Sierra to the south.

Wildflowers on slope of Mount Tallac, Desolation Wilderness

The mountains to the north are mostly volcanic, made up of rock that came out of the earth as liquid (or lava) and then solidified quickly. Volcanic rock is less durable than granite, and it is less resistant to glaciers. So when the glaciers move down canyon, they do so smoothly and evenly. Lacking the stop-and-go business with the joints, they don't dally around to scour out tarns and carve lakes.

These are not geological abstractions. The path some glacier took across this or that kind of rock 10-or-20,000 years ago has everything to do with the path we take today.

The character of the Sierra north of Sonora Pass is astonishingly gentle—at least in comparison to where we've been. The elevations drop, so we encounter far less snow. (Hence less snowmelt, hence fewer breeding pools, hence fewer mosquitoes.) The few snowfields that remain are easily navigated—cheap imitations of our past travails. The stream fords dwindle into meek trickles that we can skip across with barely a splashed sock. There are far fewer lakes (again, fewer mosquitoes). Our mileage leaps from 15 or 18 a day to 20 or 25. There is no more talk of quitting.

The biggest difference of all is the mental freedom. Liberated from the tyranny of petty annoyance, we can actually take the time to notice our surroundings. So it is now, for the first time, that I see the snowmelt-fed flowers underfoot. Carpets of them cover entire hillsides.

I mean really *see* them. Back in Yosemite, there were a few places where we climbed past rock and flower gardens on our way down into some endless plunging canyon or up to a pass high in the sky. Once or twice we defied the mosquitoes and stopped to admire them. But it's safe to say that true appreciation did not take place under those conditions.

Now it can. At a highway crossing, a Forest Service sign helpfully informs us that there are something like 200 species of wildflowers on these hillsides.

I decide to count for myself. Unfortunately, after I get up to about seven or eight, I lose track of which ones I already counted and I have to start again. This time, I divide the flowers by color. But where does red end and orange begin? What about the purple and gold daisies—if I count them as purple, will I remember not to count them as gold? This time I make it to 22 before confusion sets in.

Here, the growing season is measured not in months, but in weeks, or days. The timer starts ticking as soon as the snow melts (and in some cases, even before). From then on, the flowers are in a race with the seasons. As a result, most alpine flowers are perennials: annuals just don't have enough time to live an entire life cycle in the truncated growing season.

Another change is that now we've got plenty of company. At each pass, the parking lots are full, and within one or two miles from each trailhead, the slopes are crowded with day-hikers spending a summer Saturday toting field guides and cameras up a mountain to peer at cinquefoils and penstemons. Sometime in the last week summer vacation started for real. It's no longer just thru-hikers. But I don't mind the company. I like seeing people out doing this kind of thing— especially the senior citizens in their 70s or 80s. They show me what I want to be when I grow up.

Part of the reason for the crowds is accessibility. This is the gentle part of the Sierra. The passes are actually passable, not ridiculous notches in sky-high granite walls. There are highways here, and railroads. With all of this activity, it's hard to conceive that 150 years ago these mountains presented the same kind of obstacle to California that the Continental Divide did in Colorado or the Appalachians in pioneer America: they stopped travel and trade and thwarted the seemingly inbred American drive to migrate west.

Wandering daisy and Sierra Buttes, Plumas National Forest

Sierra Buttes, Plumas National Forest

Ponderosa pine, Bunker Hill ridge

Onion Valley Creek, Feather River National Scenic Area

In 1827, mountain-man Jedediah Smith became the first known white person to cross the Sierra. That makes European-American history here a mere 170 years old—young even for this adolescent continent. Smith arrived in these parts with an impressive wilderness dossier: In 1824, he had led the first party over South Pass in Wyoming. Shortly after, he crossed the Tehachapis in southern California. In 1827, he wanted to return east, but he needed to avoid the Spanish lands to the south, where his unapproved wanderings had irritated the local authorities. So he headed north, hoping that one or another river drainage would lead to a breach in the mountain walls. Up the Kings River—to a dead end. Up the American River; another dead end. If you are a thru-hiker, reading about these failed attempts, these pointless climbs (not to mention the wasted mileage), causes sympathetic fatigue. Finally, Smith found the Stanislaus River and crossed the ridge at or near today's Ebbetts Pass.

One last note about Smith is of particular interest to PCT thru-hikers: He walked all the way across California and Oregon, so we can claim him as our forerunner, an elder of our tribe. One minor difference between Smith and us: We have a trail to follow.

Other familiar figures in these parts included Kit Carson and John C. Fremont, who left their names all over the West, discovering this and that and performing various impossible-to-imagine feats. Here in the Sierra, they outdid themselves. They explored on snowshoes in the middle of February; ran out of most of their food; ate meals of pea soup, mule, and dog (it wouldn't have been so bad, wrote one diarist, if only they had a little salt); got lost and found; and took directions from local Indians who gave them optimistic advice like: "Rock upon rock, snow upon snow. Even if you get over the snow, you will not be able to get down from the mountains."

On February 14, 1844, Fremont and Charles Preuss, a German topographer, climbed to the summit of Red Lake Peak. This was a first ascent, and not only in the usual sense: it was the first recorded climb in the Sierra of an identifiable mountain. Another first: the sighting below of "a beautiful view of a mountain lake…so entirely surrounded by mountains that we could not discover an outlet."

It was Lake Tahoe.

You can see it from the PCT. For us, it was resupply number 12.

With a depth of 1,645 feet, Lake Tahoe is the tenth deepest lake in the world. At 195 square miles, it is the largest of the approximately 1,500 lakes and tarns in the Sierra Nevada. It used to be said that you could drop a dinner plate and still see it when it was 160 feet below the surface. You don't hear that anymore. The famously clear waters are no longer quite so pristine.

Lake Tahoe is cursed by location. Not its natural location, which is perfect, but the location of the state line, which divides over-populated, over-regulated California from under-populated, under-regulated Nevada. At the intersection is a border boomtown that is less a town than a nonstop strip mall. Annually, Lake Tahoe logs some 12 million visitor-days, about as many as Yosemite, Kings Canyon, and Sequoia National Parks put together.

There is a certain amount of culture shock that occurs when you've been living pretty much outdoors for a few weeks or months and you return to what we so thoughtlessly call civilization. I remember that as a child, I would come home from a month at summer camp, where we slept in canvas army-style tents. I would sit in my room and stare at the walls and the ceilings and think about how strange indoor air felt.

This isn't great-outdoorsperson posturing: as I believe I have made clear, Dan and I enthusiastically embrace the perks of town, especially a shower, a laundromat, and a good meal.

View of Painted Dunes from Cinder Cone, Lassen Volcanic National Park

But we just can't wrap our minds around Lake Tahoe. Friends have arranged to spend a couple of days in town visiting with us. We met Monie and Herb in Yellowstone National Park when we were hiking the Continental Divide in 1990. The retired couple from California invited us into their R.V. for drinks and snacks. You might not expect that one of the highlights of a wilderness trip is making new friends, but our experience is that if you put yourself out in the middle of the world on foot, you are going to meet a variety of people who might never even cross your path back at home: people of different backgrounds, education levels, ideologies, and ages. We've been corresponding with Monie and Herb for several years; now they're whisking us off to a restaurant in Lake Tahoe.

The meal is wonderful but the casino makes me feel like ET. One-armed bandits are plying their trade with a maximum of blinking lights and clanking bells. The lights make my eyes twitch. There is too much going on too close to my face. I keep seeing our reflections in mirrors, and I wonder if I look as strange to other people as I feel.

July 17. Day 73. Mile 1,100. Desolation Wilderness.

I sometimes think that the places with the most negative-sounding place names are the most beautiful. Go somewhere called the Devil's Staircase, Devil's Racecourse, Hell's Canyon, Devil's Thumb (finger, arm, head, or profile), and you're practically guaranteed a spectacular walk.

Our first night in the Desolation Wilderness, and it's as beautiful as the name led me to expect: craggy and lake-dotted with views reminiscent of the High Sierra. After all the noise and activity of Lake Tahoe, I am glad to be in the backcountry again. The silence is expansive. The only flashing lights are the twinkling stars. We're back where we belong.

—DAN'S JOURNAL

The Desolation Wilderness gets its name courtesy of the glaciers, which deposited a rubble-field of durable rock on the landscape. Trees have a hard time growing on granite, hence there are fewer of them than might ordinarily be expected at this elevation. But that hardly makes this a wilderness of desolation. Each inviting tarn hosts a fisherman or two. The trail is gentle. Plus, how desolate can it be? This wilderness boasts the densest population of hikers per square mile of any roadless area in California.

Statistics can be misleading. The area's hiker density does not mean that backpackers are stacked cheek by jowl in barren-earthed campsites. The vast majority —by, as far as I could tell, about a factor of 100 to 1—that we saw in the Desolation Wilderness were day-hiking, not backpacking, and the vast majority of the day-hikers were within one mile of a trailhead.

Farther north, the concentration of day-hikers is even higher, and it reaches its apex near Donner Pass, where I don't think I would be exaggerating if I claimed that we saw 200 hikers within four miles of the pass, and 100 cars at the trailhead. At one point, Dan and I had to stand and wait our turn for 10 minutes while a group of 30 slid and stumbled across a snowfield, giggling and shrieking and generally acting like they were on an amusement park ride. When Dan and I finally crossed, the entire traverse took us a few seconds. At times like this, we are acutely aware of the difference that has developed between us as thru-hikers and everyone else. It's the wilderness that is our home now, the place where we look and feel like we belong.

Donner Pass, however, is not wilderness. The trailhead is bubbling with the activity and conversation of happy vacationers and frolicking children.

But in my mind I hear different voices, because this is a pass with a history and a story to tell.

Hiking and history seem to go together in the West, perhaps because so much of western history is tied to the crossing and exploration of the great mountain ranges. Reading about Lewis and Clark or the early mountain men or the settlers of the Oregon Trail, I almost always hear in their words echoes of my own experience.

In one important respect, any comparison is superficial: our hike of the Pacific Crest Trail is a luxury. Any hardships are voluntary. Given average weather conditions, we can bail out anywhere and within a

KAREN SIGNING TRAIL REGISTER
AT LASSEN VOLCANIC NATIONAL PARK

few days—sometimes, within a few hours—we can be in a motel in front of a television feasting on take-out pizza. The ever-present safety net of civilization changes the nature of our experience, just like a safety net changes the nature of a high-wire act.

Still, there are some similarities. The settlers would recognize the questions that consume our attention: How far can we walk? How much food is in our packs? Where will we get water? What if the weather turns? Will we make it before winter? Should we take the more dangerous, faster high route or the safer, slower low route?

So, Donner Pass.

In 1846, two brothers—Illinois farmers in their 60s—headed west with their families to the greener pastures of California. They crossed South Pass in Wyoming; somewhere along the way they learned of an alternate route called the Hastings Cutoff. The Donner brothers became the leaders of a party of 91 people who broke off to take the shortcut.

Well, what thru-hiker wouldn't understand that? Winter was coming. The Hastings Cutoff was 200 miles shorter than the traditional route. Other parties had used it successfully.

The cutoff was a disaster. Having lost their way, the party had to cut 36 miles of trail in the Wasatch mountains. Many of their cattle and oxen, which they relied on to pull the wagon and for food, died in the Great Salt Lake Desert. When they finally got back on the trail, their 200 mile shortcut had put them three weeks behind schedule and short of food.

When Dan and I arrive at Donner Pass, our food sacks, too, are empty. We, however, are expecting to meet our friend Cameron here for a picnic and resupply. Cameron had originally intended to join us for the High Sierra, but a foot injury thwarted his hiking plans. Instead, he has met us at a couple of road crossings with a pickup truck full of food. He's relying on his own knowledge of backpacking (actually, he said that he's relying on his own backpacking food fantasies) to figure out what to bring. But after several hours of waiting, it becomes clear that something has gone wrong.

For the past few days, we've been traveling in the general vicinity of two young men, Will and Jason. We've invited them to join us at the anticipated feast. When Cameron doesn't arrive, they immediately set to rifling through their food bags, claiming that they have extra of this, enough of that. But before we take them up on their offer, Cameron finally shows up. A miscommunication had him waiting for us at the wrong road crossing.

But returning to the Donner Party, who in 1846 waited for a delivery of food, but under radically different circumstances. Having realized that there weren't enough supplies to get over the pass, they polled their party for volunteers to go ahead, cross the mountains, and return with provisions. Two members of the group answered the call, leaving the Donner brothers and the rest of the party behind. Only one of them was able to complete the mission. By the time he did, snow was already on the ground.

They might still have made it. Huddled somewhere down on the eastern side of the pass, they went over their options: Do we push ahead, or hang back? Do we hope for a break in the weather, or assume that the winter is here to stay? The urge to rest must have been strong—but was it stronger than the urge to be done with the ordeal? They probably thought it through, argued, made the best decision they knew how to make. It was the wrong one.

Rather than attacking the pass immediately, the party took a few days off to rest. An early storm came in and made travel impossible. The winter settled in and the rest is grim history. The settlers tried to cross the pass three times, got lost, and ran out of food. Finally they resorted to cannibalism. Of 91 people, 49 survived.

One book on the Donner party tragedy has a cover picture of people struggling up a steep rock-and-snow-strewn hillside. But in summer, the pass looks flat and gentle. The temperature is easily 90 degrees. It's impossible to imagine this as the killer terrain that forced settlers into cannibalism and despair.

But it did, and I wonder: Would I—super-tough thru-hiker who can bound across a snowfield that sends lesser mortals into paroxysms of fear—have been strong enough to survive? Are we really as at-home in the wilderness as we think we are?

Lassen Peak and Hat Creek Rim, Lassen National Forest

Ghost trees near Hat Creek

Waterfall, Burney Falls State Park

Old-growth forest near Butcherknife Creek, Shasta National Forest

When, later in the day, we regroup at the I-80 rest stop, Cameron has assembled the following spread on the picnic table: A barbecue grill, a two-burner stove, two coolers, steaks, hamburgers, fresh fruits and vegetables, salad fixings, cold cuts, condiments, a pizza, bread and rolls, beer, wine, soda, juice, cappuccino, Gatorade, candy, and strawberry-rhubarb pie.

Our meal, it must be said, lacks historical authenticity.

We are at a point in our hike where the days seem to melt into one another. They are fast days, for sure: the terrain is easy, and our mileage is edging up. But they are also undifferentiated. The landscape is pretty enough—if it were in the East, have no doubt that it would be trumpeted as a vast and untrammeled wilderness.

But it's not the East, it's the West. We know western wilderness, and this isn't it. We have moved into multiple use lands, laced with roads. The character of our hike has changed.

The change is not overwhelming; certainly nothing so dramatic as the show-off geology at Sonora Pass. A road here, another road there, some of them attached to logging operations. But it is hard to feel like the king of the wild frontier when your frontier keeps bumping up against parking lots. And on a practical note, it is hard to accept the multiple-use gospel that hikers can share forests with loggers when the latter's clearcuts destroy the streams and springs we depend on.

In 1945, PCT visionary Clinton Clarke wrote a book called *Pacific Crest Trailways*, in which he characterized each area the trail was to pass through. Even back then, this part of northern California elicited concern. "To keep this a wilderness and protect it from the ever-constant encroachment of roads and recreation development will require active vigilance and determination. Conditions are critical and hard work only can preserve this matchless region."

DEER, TRINITY ALPS WILDERNESS

The sound of off-road vehicles, the jeep tracks, the bellowing cows munching their way through the riparian vegetation are sad evidence that he was right.

The trail itself follows a meandering route that has more to do with property boundaries than trail sense. On our way into Sierra City, we pass an abundance of hand-lettered signs saying things like "Double Bar-O Claim, no trespassing," which evoke the region's past as 49ers gold rush country. Gold fever still runs, although it's tepid, not high. You can buy a mechanical gold panner from Sears and Roebuck that will work your claim, and as we walk along, we see several panners chugging along in the riverbeds.

July 22. Day 78. Mile 1,191. Sierra City.

This isn't hiker country. Even in town, there's a distinct feeling that hikers are entirely peripheral to anything important. There's a sign asking us not to congregate on the bench outside the store because that's where the regulars eat their lunch. The guy who owns the hotel across the street wouldn't allow one hiker, who had rented a room, to let another hiker use his shower, even though they asked permission and offered to pay. Nobody cares that you've walked here from Mexico. Not that they should; *it's just that people usually do. Generosity and interest are so common in most towns near the trail that when you find a community that just doesn't care, it seems surprising.*

—DAN'S JOURNAL

Perhaps it is the lack of significant landmarks with which to measure our progress. Perhaps it is simply that after all this time, we have yet to cross a state line. But for the last week or so, it has felt as though we are walking in place.

In Sierra City, we pass the time doing mental arithmetic while waiting for our laundry to dry.

• We have been walking a total of 78 days (including all our days off, and time out for resupplies) and have covered 1,191 miles.

• Our average daily mileage has therefore been a paltry 15.3 miles a day.

• We are *still* in California.

• It is still 501 miles by trail to the Oregon border.

• If we hike the rest of the trail at the same pace, we will reach Canada on October 20.

A little voice is telling us that we must go faster.

There is a way to do it. Cameron has offered to slackpack us for a week, starting at our next town stop in Belden.

Slackpacking is hiker slang for hiking without a pack. A friend takes your pack at a road crossing. You hike on while he or she drives to another road crossing farther up the trail. At night, you either camp with your support person, or you get in a few more miles by retrieving your pack, walking on, and camping in the backcountry. The next morning, you meet up again. Obviously, this only works in an area with plenty of roads.

Slackpacking will allow us to increase our pace to 30 miles a day. This is monotonous terrain, and with all the roads and multiple-use activities, it is not a wilderness experience; there are no flowers to slow down and smell. Not every mile of a long-distance trail can be spectacular, and the miles here aren't. It's a good place to fly.

It might sound like all we want to do is get the hike over and done with, but that's not the point. The point is that we want to be *able* to finish. Remember the Donner party? Sometime in October, winter will come to the North Cascades and the trail will become impassable. There's no way to tell exactly when the door to the highcountry will slam shut, but the earlier in October we can arrive, the better our chances will be.

Moonrise, Castle Crags State Park

The 90 miles between Sierra City and Belden continue in pretty much the same vein. The trail undulates across the lay of the land. Approaching the northern end of the Sierra Nevada, the elevations are getting lower. In the High Sierra, we would have had to dig a well to get to 7,000 feet; now, 7,000 feet marks the high points of the ridges and passes. The low points are getting lower, too. The Middle Fork of the Feather River, elevation 2,900 feet, is the lowest we have been since Agua Dulce, 828 miles ago. It is mid-summer now, and with the lower elevations come higher temperatures and drier terrain; many of the seasonal springs and streams are starting to dry up.

Belden, elevation 2,310, is a good place for a town stop, if you can call it a town. It's a well-equipped trailer park, with a bar, a general store, a post office the size of a New York City apartment bathroom, a laundry room, a restroom with shower facilities, and a few cabins for rent. At the bar, you can buy hamburger meat and the right to cook it on an outdoor grill on a porch overlooking the North Fork of the Feather River. Those amenities, a weekly potluck dinner, and the fact that everything is about a one minute walk from everything else make Belden the perfect thru-hiker pit stop. At 10:00 on Sunday morning, the bar is open and it's business as usual—which means that most of the barstools are occupied.

Cameron meets us as planned and we leave town feeling weightless without our packs. It's a good thing, too, because the first order of business is a 5,500 foot climb, which means that pretty much every step we take for the next 10 hours is going to be uphill.

On our second day of slackpacking, we find a note that a fellow hiker has left on the trail under a rock. Thru-hikers have been communicating with each other this way all along the trail, sharing information about water sources or campsites or hiking plans or good places to eat in town. This note tells us that we have reached the halfway point of the hike, and adds the editorial comment that this means that everything we've just done, we have to do all over again.

For the next couple of miles, I chew on that. What we have so far done seems so colossal that I can barely fit it into my brain; that we have to do it all over again is unimaginable. It strikes me as interesting that when we meet other thru-hikers, even the most experienced and enthusiastic of them seem taken aback by this reality. No one is saying, "Oh, good, look at how much is still ahead." I think it's partly because of our fear of winter and partly because lately we've all felt a little like we've been swimming in molasses. We're ready for something new.

And the trail obliges.

After 800 miles, we are finally leaving the Sierra Nevada. Shimmering in front of us, welcoming us to the fiery peaks of the Cascade Range, is Mount Lassen, the first of the great volcanoes, which will be our beacons from now until we reach the Canadian border.

Extending from Lassen to the Frazer River in British Columbia, the Cascades are part of a global structure called the Pacific ring of volcanoes. In addition to the volcanoes of the Pacific Northwest, the ring includes mountains in the Andes, the Aleutian Islands, Japan, Indonesia, New Zealand and Antarctica.

The volcanoes exist because of plate tectonics. The Pacific plate—think of a big dish floating on the earth's liquid magma, far beneath the Pacific Ocean—is expanding, and as it does, it pushes against the continental plates, exacerbating volcanic activity. Switch images for a minute and picture a car crashing into the back of a truck. The Pacific plate is the car; the impact of the crash pushes it down, under the truck's fender. When the Pacific plate (the car) is pushed down, it gets closer to the hot and molten core of the earth and is exposed to extreme heat. Matter melts into magma, which is fed into the volcanoes, which, cannonlike, shoot it out of the earth. Hence the ring of fire-breathing mountains.

At least that's what geologists think.

The Indian tribes of the Pacific Northwest, having been spared Geology 101, had their own explanation: volcanoes are gods. Like our familiar pantheon of Greek and Roman gods, they engage in a never ending series of petty rivalries and feuds, and when they're not angry at each other, they get angry at humans. The Greek gods threw lightning bolts and created tidal waves; the volcanic gods throw fire.

Moonset over Peak 7550, Marble Mountain Wilderness

The Indians, always better than European-Americans at naming mountains, called Lassen "the sweathouse of the gods." Just inside the border of Lassen Volcanic National Park, Boiling Springs Lake gives solid evidence of the area's volcanic activity. Indeed, before Mount St. Helens erupted in 1980, Lassen was the most recent of the major volcanic peaks to erupt in the Pacific Northwest. Starting in 1914, it erupted on and off for seven years. It's the only 10,000-foot volcano in the Cascades that is not a stratovolcano; instead, it is a plug dome volcano, which means that it contains no non-volcanic matter. It was formed as a vent on the north side of a larger volcano named Tehama, which blew itself up. Lassen is an important study area for volcanologists, and we chat with two of them who are on their way to the lake. It's obvious that it would make their day if the gods that inhabit the sweathouse would imminently engage in one of their temper tantrums. Unfortunately (for volcanologists with cars) or fortunately (for hikers on foot), the danger is pretty slim. As geologist Bates McKee points out, "From an actuarial point of view, even active volcanoes are infinitely safer than are highways."

It's far more reasonable—if less dramatic—to worry about falling through the heat-softened earth into one of the sulfurous fumaroles and mud pots surrounding the lake. You can smell them long before you see them; long before you hear them bubbling and burbling and steaming and hissing. Considering that the geyser activity in Lassen Volcanic National Park is second in the contiguous United States only to that in Yellowstone National Park, it seems surprising that aside from the volcanologists, no one is on the trail or near the lake to see these natural wonders.

Lassen is a small park. The entire hike through it takes only a day. We're doing ridiculous mileage now: 33, 30, 28 miles a day. My feet are feeling the strain, although the anti-inflammatories I'm taking continue to keep the heel pain under control. Some of the younger hikers maintain this kind of mileage on a routine basis, and I just don't see how they do it. Even after 1,000 miles on the trail, even without the weight of a pack, I find the last few miles of a 30-mile day excruciatingly long and slow.

North of Lassen, the trail returns to a mediocre route. The forests are timber farms: monocultural, even-aged stands of lumber-in-the-making. About once every mile, the trail crosses a road. There are plenty of campsites, but not cozy little alcoves that give hikers the cocooned feeling of a home in the woods. These are the kind of bare-earthed sites that come furnished with sitting logs and wooden tables and contraptions that I assume you'd use to hang and gut a fresh-killed deer. The fire rings are incinerators: 2 feet tall, 4 feet wide, filled with half-burnt cans and paper packaging. The up-side is that it's easy to find a place to camp when we meet up at night with Cameron and the pickup truck.

Ahead of us is the infamous Hat Creek Rim, a dry, hot escarpment that, due to private property issues and a lack of water, has been a headache for trail planners and hikers alike. After that, it's the timber country northwest of Burney Falls State Park.

Although we are by air not more than 95 miles from the Oregon border, the trail now appears to have decided that we haven't yet seen enough of California. So instead of continuing due north and taking us into Oregon where we can celebrate the achievement of walking across America's third largest state, we're now headed west, to the Klamath Mountains. It's going to take us another 275 miles to get to Oregon!

The reason is water, or a lack thereof, which made a route due north along the main ridge of the Cascades unfeasible. There were other challenges, too. As Clinton Clarke observed in 1945, the area is characterized by "private lands, lumbered regions, and commercialized areas. Not much can be done about this."

Hayes Creek, Marble Mountain Wilderness

View of Upper Sky Lake and Marble Mountain from Shadow Lake, Marble Mountain Wilderness

In Burney, a ranger from the Shasta-Trinity National Forest stops to chat with us. He recognizes us immediately as thru-hikers.

"You guys going northbound or southbound?" he asks.

The question elicits a real sense of accomplishment: you have to be pretty far along for someone to wonder which way you're going.

"Northbound," we say.

"Crap country up there," he tells us. "A real mess. I'm glad I don't have to walk through it."

The problem, he says, is lack of funds for maintenance. The area is sparsely populated, and many of the people who do live there work for timber companies, so there's no base of volunteers to maintain the trails.

Actually, I don't quite agree with the ranger. This isn't crap country. It's actually prime habitat for *Abies magnifica*, one of the largest firs in the world, found almost exclusively in northern California and southern Oregon. The red fir is the dominant tree of the upper montane zone; it's also a mainstay of the local economy. From a clear-cutter's perspective, it's just about the perfect tree because it's big and easy to harvest. The short growing season prevents deciduous trees from growing alongside it and cluttering up the loggers' path. Similarly, the gentle, unglaciated landscape here is easier to log than craggy glaciated terrain. Unfortunately, these forests don't easily regenerate, and they have been logged throughout the century. In 1901, Muir wrote:

> *Over nearly all of the more accessible slopes . . . at a height of from three to six thousand feet above the sea, and for a distance of about 600 miles, the waste and confusion extends. Happy robbers! Dwelling in the most beautiful woods . . . roses and lilies at their feet . . . as if cheering them on in their desolating work. There is none to say them nay.*

The first clearcuts are startling in their violence. No matter how many times I see a clearcut, I'm always surprised by the totality of the destruction. It's like a giant was playing pick-up-sticks and refused to put away his toys. And it's hard to accept the Forest Service's plea of poverty regarding funds for trail maintenance when there's obviously plenty of money to build logging roads that are virtually backwoods highways; certainly the logging truck drivers seem to think they are as they speed by snorting fumes.

Fortunately, at 30 miles a day, you don't stay anywhere very long. When we arrive at Castle Crags State Park, near Interstate 5 and Dunsmuir, the great mileage marathon is finally over. Here, the trail goes back into more remote country—including the Castle Crags, Trinity Alps, Marble Mountain, and Russian wildernesses—so Cameron will leave, and we'll again shoulder our packs. We have covered 216 miles in seven days.

August 5. Day 91. Mile 1,500. Castle Crags State Park.

Castle Crags State Park seems empty without Milt Kenney, who died a few years ago. I remember a strong but gentle man, whose muscles rippled from a lifetime as a lumberjack, but whose heart was soft as butter. On my 1986 hike, I spent four nights here because this trail angel par excellence was so nice to us. Every day, he drove us from our campsite at the park into town for various errands. He showed up with snacks and invited us to dinner.

CAMPSITE NEAR BEAR LAKE

I think he helped hundreds of hikers on their way just for the pleasure of being part of their journey. I remember his daughter telling me that after his wife died, he felt empty until he found the trail community. After that, he used to be like a kid at Christmas, waiting for the thru-hiking season to start. What he seemed to enjoy most was having us accompany him to local softball games. Driving into town today we passed the ball field and I felt a pang.

This year, Milt's daughter Adele is carrying on the tradition in memory of her father. She has been shuttling hikers all over everywhere, even to Mount Shasta. A few of the PCT thru-hikers are making it a point to climb some of the big volcanoes.

—DAN'S JOURNAL

Shasta is imposing: a dominating hunk that you can see no matter where you go. Already, it seems to be a permanent fixture on our horizon. Muir called it "a colossal cone rising in solitary grandeur and might well be regarded as an object of religious worship." Others, apparently, agree. The mountain has attracted a truly impressive collection of cults, all convinced of the mountain's divine importance. Perhaps the most interesting legend concerns the Lemurians, thought to live in underground tunnels. The Lemurians (so say people who claim to have met them) are refugees from the Kingdom of Mu (the Atlantis of the Pacific); a highly evolved people who are seven feet tall with a nut-sized organ in the middle of their foreheads that allows them to communicate by ESP.

I wish we could climb Shasta; I really do. I would love to stand that high above the landscape, and visit whichever Lemurians happened to be out and about that day. But we can't succumb to the temptation. The task at hand is the trail to the north, and the days are ticking away.

From Castella, we have a 5,500-foot climb through desert-like chaparral during a heat wave. Shades of southern California! The climb is long and arduous, but there's nothing new about that. Anyway, I'm not tempted to whine about working hard when at every turn of the trail I'm rewarded with views of something as grand and dramatic as Castle Crags. The granitic domes and pinnacles are reminiscent of the rock formations near Mount Whitney in the High Sierra. After so many miles of indifferent terrain, the spectacle seems almost shocking.

We're still pushing the mileage, averaging 20 miles a day. (What is troublesome, however, is that we are heading west, not north.) The terrain is vastly improved. The Marble Mountains and the Trinity Alps are worth a place on any backpacker's to-do list. And they apparently are, judging from the crowds.

For the first time, some of the hikers we are meeting are southbound thru-hikers. Not many, though: the harsh winter of the Pacific Northwest cut the number of southbounders down to a mere handful. All of them have snowy tales to tell of the fearsome North Cascades.

The last few days to Oregon are one big push. The trail follows a ridgeline route, and there's nothing to complain about except a lack of water. Sometimes we drop down to lakes so that we can drink and swim. Sometimes we get lucky and reach a campsite at the end of the day. And sometimes we simply carry water and carve out a flat spot wherever darkness happens to find us. The last category comprises an eclectic and not always attractive collection: a gravel bar near a road, a brushy shelf above a creek, a barely flat patch of dirt at a trail junction, a closed campground. One of the springs we intended to use has a salt block in it. Many we share with cattle. It's not that there aren't good campsites—there are. But we can't stop in the middle of the day to use them.

Mileage, mileage, mileage.

August 11. Day 98. Mile 1,631. Cold Springs Creek.

Almost there. Today, we saw Oregon for the first time. Of course, it doesn't look any different than California. But according to our maps, Oregon is only a few miles to the north, and from Buckborn Ridge, we had a clear and endless view. I think I know how the settlers of the Oregon Trail felt.

—Dan's journal

Seiad Valley is our last stop in California. As we walk into town, snacking on perfectly ripe blackberries, we disturb two bears doing the same thing. Actually, they're not picking berries as much as they are inhaling them. Bears don't eat berries like you and I do. Putting a bear in a berry patch is sort of like putting a vacuum cleaner in there: branches, leaves, berries, all go into the mouth; what the bear doesn't want gets spit back out. It's a noisy and inelegant process.

According to basic bear protocol, the last thing you're supposed to do is mess with a feeding bear. They get grumpy when their meals are interrupted. But here there's no way to avoid it: blackberry bushes are everywhere, and in order for us to get past the bears, they are going to have to move, since they have the advantage of thick skin and fur and can bash their way through a blackberry tangle. Fortunately, all parties concerned seem to favor mutual avoidance. We stop picking berries and the bears retreat into the woods. On all sides, a civilized solution.

At Seiad Valley, the owner of the cafe has a wager to offer thru-hikers: If you can eat all of his "pancake challenge" breakfast, you get it for free.

The challenge is a stack of five 1-inch-thick, 12-inch-diameter pancakes. It's a proposition thru-hikers can't seem to resist. Dan's eyes are glittering with anticipation until he learns that Kirk and Conrad, two thru-hikers from Michigan we met a few days back, split the platter between them and still couldn't finish it. A young man going by the trail name Captain Marcus shows up and falls victim to the pancake platter. So do two southbounders, who, hearing about the challenge from northbounders, have fasted for two days in preparation. During the time we're in Seiad Valley, the score is something like Pancake Platter: 5; Thru-hikers: 0.

But you can't argue that by the time we leave the valley for the last push into Oregon, everyone is well-fueled to tackle California's final climb. When, 35.4 miles later, we arrive at a small marker that tells us we have reached the Oregon border on the PCT, I feel a couple of tears trickling down my cheeks.

We have been walking 101 days and have covered 1,692.4 miles. We have 966.3 to go.

Smith Lake and Mount Shasta, Klamath National Forest

Dawn light on Crater Lake, Crater Lake National Park

OREGON: THE PROMISED LAND

Between 1843 and 1868, some 350,000 emigrants packed all they could carry and set out from Independence, Missouri, for the western valleys of Oregon, half a continent and 2,000 miles away.

Over the 25-year period of the great westward migration, more than 75,000 covered wagons etched a dusty path so deep into the earth that ruts from their wheels still scar the land today. Some emigrants rode horses, some sat in wagons. Most adults, however, walked, preferring to use precious wagon space for food and house-hold goods. The pace was 15–20 miles a day, a pace not unlike ours.

The differences: On the Oregon trail—the real one—there were no rest days in town, no care packages from home, no opportunity to quit the trail when things got hard, no way to turn back. Also, on that other Oregon Trail, it is estimated there is a grave every one-tenth of a mile.

During the westward migration, Oregon country (as it was called) extended east clear to Wyoming. When the settlers crossed the Oregon border (what is today the Idaho-Wyoming border), they still had 800 miles to go.

But they had done 1,200 miles, and I imagine they were feeling at least a little feisty about it. They had crossed the dusty plains of Kansas and Nebraska, climbed up and over the Continental Divide, and survived the waterless western drylands. Now, they were on a downhill run. The rivers were Pacific-bound and so were they. I think I know how they felt.

Oregon. The promised land.

Like a skilled and attentive host, Oregon hits the perfect note right from the start. Our first campsite is furnished with a piped spring of sparkling water (in contrast to the cattle-contaminated mudholes that passed for springs our last few nights in California). The forests seem a little denser, the temperature a tad cooler. When Mount Shasta, which has been dominating the horizon for more than two weeks, finally recedes and disappears behind us, we know that we have really and truly left California.

Ashland, just over the border, is our first resupply and the largest town since Lake Tahoe. As we enter the confusing sprawl, the roads and buildings overwhelm our forest-muted sensibilities. But a friendly young woman stops to give us directions and ends up offering us a ride. "Welcome to Ashland," she tells us. "You'll like it; it's a great town."

She's right; we do and it is.

August 15. Day 102. Mile 1,721. Ashland.

Like Lake Tahoe, Ashland is a tourist mecca—but in a different mold. Here, people show up carrying tickets for the Shakespeare Festival, instead of a bucket of nickels for the gambling machines. We managed to snag tickets for "Timon of Athens"—Saturday night, 10th row center. The restaurants feature ethnic cuisines like Thai and Indian; the grocery store is a gourmet's delight; and no matter what food you choose you can wash it down with local microbrew. There's a choice of ale or stout, flavors like honey wheat or raspberry, filtered or unfiltered, and a whole bunch of concoctions I don't even recognize as beer.

In every way I can think of, this is a town stop to savor—especially if you consider that the next one is 429 miles away, in Cascade Locks, on the Washington border.

—Dan's journal

Leaving Ashland, our first task is to get back east to the main range of the Cascades. For the first couple of days, the trail in Oregon is more businesslike than attractive, taking us through a hodgepodge of multiple-use lands.

But once we rejoin the Cascades, the trail begins to follow the gentle, lyrical route that will be typical of its traverse from here on in.

Gentle does not mean boring.

Look, for instance, at the path the Oregon PCT takes around the volcanic giants. In California, we circled around Lassen and Shasta without ever really meeting them up close and personal. Here, there's none of that worship-from-afar, look-but-don't-touch business. We're going to walk on the flanks of these peaks, step on their lava beds, and cross their glacier-fed streams. From now almost through the end of our trip, great volcanoes will appear on the northern horizon, draw us north, then recede behind us as we set our sights on the next beacon ahead.

Mount McLoughlin, elevation 9,493 feet, is the first. It's the only mountain I know of that's been named for a purveyor of trail magic. Originally called Mount Pitt, the peak was renamed in honor of one Dr. John McLoughlin, an employee of the Hudson's Bay Company, who dispensed his version of trail magic to the settlers of the Oregon Trail. At a time when both the United States and England claimed parts of the Oregon Territory—and almost came to blows over the location of the Canadian-American border—McLoughlin was famous for aiding all comers.

From Mount McLoughlin north, hikers face several choices of route. The now defunct Oregon Skyline Trail is the ancestor of Oregon's Pacific Crest Trail. Originally running from Crater Lake in the south of the state to Mount Hood in the north, the Oregon Skyline Trail was extended on both ends to reach the borders of California and Washington. The final California-to-Washington footway was completed in 1937, thus becoming one of the earliest major links of the PCT. Today, much of the old route has been abandoned in favor of the PCT's current, higher route, but segments of the OST still exist and are maintained as trails in individual forests and wilderness areas.

Despite its name, the Oregon Skyline Trail frequently stayed at lower elevations than today's PCT. One of the reasons trail managers put the PCT on its higher, drier route was to establish a more truly crest-line path. The other was to avoid contributing to problems of overuse at popular lakeside campsites. Sometimes, they succeeded too well: the PCT in the Sky Lakes Wilderness manages the seemingly impossible feat of avoiding almost all of the wilderness's namesake lakes and ponds.

North of the Sky Lakes Wilderness, the terrain gets even drier as the trail crosses the so-called Oregon Desert, a landscape that is not so much a desert as it is a semiarid sandy-soiled forest of scraggly looking lodgepole pines. There's plenty of water here. Unfortunately for hikers, almost all of it is underground, buried by volcanic deposits of porous pumice and ash.

The culprit is a mountain named Mazama.

You won't see Mount Mazama on any map of Oregon, but it's the next big volcano on our route. Or, rather, what's left of it.

What's left is a 20.25-square-mile hole in the ground now filled with water. With a depth of 1,932 feet, Crater Lake is the deepest lake in the United States and the seventh-deepest lake in the world.

The mountain was originally one of the great volcanoes of the Pacific Northwest, probably about 12,000-feet tall, which would make it as high as present-day Mount Adams. When it erupted circa 4900 B.C.,

the explosion had 40 times the force of the 1980 explosion of Mount St. Helens. We tend to think of geological phenomena of this magnitude as events that occurred long before humans came into the picture. But 4900 B.C. is practically yesterday in geological terms, and it's certainly within the scope of human settlement in North America. Native Americans living nearby probably would have witnessed the explosion.

The volcano spewed 42 cubic miles of matter and covered 350,000 square miles, including much of Oregon and Washington, as well as parts of Nevada, Idaho, Montana, Wyoming, Utah, British Columbia, Alberta, and even Saskatchewan, with ash. (However, very little ash made it to nearby California; the prevailing winds were from the south and west). The land at the base of the mountain was buried under 20 feet of ash; 70 miles away, a foot-deep blanket covered the ground. At the end of it all, the volcano had disintegrated; the mountain was completely gone, except for the leftover crater and Wizard Island, a small plug dome that now pokes up in the middle of the lake.

Eventually, snow and rain filled the crater and formed the lake. The crater walls tower as much as 2,000 feet over the water level. There is no outlet. The only way water escapes is through evaporation. In recent times, evaporation and precipitation have almost exactly balanced each other out. Despite the fact that the lake is nearly 2,000 feet deep, its water level rarely fluctuates by more than an inch.

A national park, Crater Lake boasts campgrounds, a lodge, and a restaurant. The motel at Mazama Campground has vacancies, and the restaurant has thoughtfully placed a menu in our room.

The choice is either to go to the restaurant and feast on such delicacies as salad, stuffed mushrooms, and fresh salmon (culinary confirmation that we're indeed in the Pacific Northwest), or to prepare our usual camp fare (macaroni and cheese, doctored with a can of tuna, freeze-dried vegetables, Parmesan cheese, and a healthy dose of Louisiana hot sauce).

Now, it's not like I have anything against mac and cheese—or any of our other backcountry meals. *Au contraire*. If you were to eavesdrop on our before-dinner conversations, you would most likely hear something like this:

Me: "What's for dinner?" (Dan usually picks. He carries more weight than I do, so it's only fair that he gets the option to unload the heaviest meals first. Also, since we're ultimately going to eat everything, I don't much care which order we do it in.)

Dan: "Mac and cheese."

Me: "Oh, goody."

Here are some variations on the conversation. Variation one:

Dan: "Stove-top stuffing and chicken."

Me: "Oh, goody."

Variation two:

Dan: "Spaghetti and tomato sauce."

Me: "Oh, goody."

Variation three:

Dan: "Potatoes, salmon, and gravy."

Me: "Oh, goody."

Whatever the menu, one thing is constant. In all the nights I've spent in the backcountry (I have no idea how many that is, but it's easily a four-digit number) I have never failed to utterly appreciate just about anything that's ever been set down before me. That doesn't, however, mean that I've lost my mind, or every last vestige of civilized sensibility. So off to the restaurant we head. We might not be the best-dressed diners making our way there, but I have no doubt that we're going to be the most appreciative.

On our way to dinner we pass an overlook at the crater's rim, and I walk over to get a better view of the lake.

"Where are you going?" Dan asks. "The lodge is the other way."

"I'm going to the overlook."

"But you'll be walking along the rim all day tomorrow and we have a dinner reservation right now," Dan reasonably points out.

Pilot Rock, Siskiyou Mountains

Easy for him to be reasonable—he saw the lake on his last PCT hike. But I don't want to wait until tomorrow to see a place our guidebook compares to the Grand Canyon.

Well, that turns out to be a little bit of an exaggeration. Comparisons often are. But Crater Lake has a beauty and magic entirely its own. The sun is slanted low, and the rock cliffs are starting to reflect the golden glints of alpenglow; the blue water looks saturated as a sapphire. Crater Lake is one of those eye-rubbing places where you keep double-checking to confirm that you really saw what you think you saw: that the cliffs really are that precipitous, that the water really is that blue, that we are, in fact, looking 1,000 feet down into the exploded guts of a gigantic volcano. It is not like anything I have ever seen before.

Interesting tidbit here: In traditional Native American cultures of the area, the local shamen forbade people to gaze upon the lake, which may explain why the Indians never got around to telling white people about it. The lake thus wasn't discovered by European-Americans until 1853, when prospectors stumbled upon it. As it turns out, it's a good thing we did take the time to look at the lake before dinner, because if we hadn't, we would have joined the long list of people who never gazed upon these mesmerizing waters.

August 19. Day 106. Mile 1,829. Mazama Village at Crater Lake.

I wonder what it is about the lake that gives it such a magnetic aura. It is said that staying here for a few days does funny things to people, although no one is very specific about what those funny things are. Well, here's one: just before dinner, we walked to the overlook because Karen said she didn't want to wait until tomorrow. When we got there I forgot all about dinner. I wanted to stay there staring at the lake and watch the blue turn deeper shades as the sun dropped lower in the sky. A thru-hiker forgetting about a restaurant meal is something that can only be attributable to supernatural forces, so I guess I can claim to have been officially bewitched.

—Dan's journal

Splat. Dribble dribble drip. Splat.

Half awake, I struggle to place the noise. It's familiar somehow, but not familiar enough to identify. It takes a while before we figure out what it is.

Rain.

In 106 days of hiking we have so far had a handful of nighttime sprinkles, one 15-minute downpour, and one soggy evening. The last real rain—the soggy evening—was on July 8 in Yosemite's Virginia Canyon. It is now August 20.

This is not something you can reasonably complain about. With all of the environmental challenges the Pacific Crest Trail has thrown our way, rain hasn't been one of them—which is why I don't even recognize the sound of it.

This particular storm seems intent on making up for a summer's worth of drought. We're talking an open-the-heavens, cats-and-dogs downpour.

We respond to the unfamiliar feel of rain on skin as if we've been slapped: "Ouch! What was that!"

We handle our rain jackets and pack covers like strange pieces of equipment we never expected to use. Along the entire western side of Crater Lake, we never once catch even a glimpse of the magic waters.

But even in a storm, Oregon again lives up to its billing as the promised land. The downpour lasts only about half a day before it turns to a light drizzle. And there is respite within easy reach: Diamond Lake Lodge, our next resupply.

Back in California, resupplying almost always meant going into towns. But here in Oregon, there are few towns near the trail. Also, we don't really need full-fledged town stops. We're not battling the in-your-face extremes of heat and snow and long waterless traverses that in California sometimes sent us scurrying into town like front-line troops in need of R and R. Here, we just need to replenish our food sacks and keep walking. That need is met by a handful of backcountry lodges near the trail, whose proprietors agree to hold hiker mail-drops, sometimes for a small fee.

Island Lake and Mount McLoughlin, Sky Lake Wilderness Area

The lodges seem like little outposts of civilization. Each is different. Some have well-stocked stores; others only carry small selections of junk food and fishing lures. Some offer pay-showers, some have restaurants. and sometimes there are public pay phones; othertimes, you pay the owner $1 a minute to use a cell-phone. What they all have in common is a certain sense of remoteness. Even at a large, well-stocked, crowded place like Diamond Lake, the disconnecting shock of leaving the wilderness for town is largely absent. There are no streetlights, no traffic; no busy, bulging stores.

Most of our food drops in Oregon are quickies: stop, resupply, eat a meal, and keep walking. Diamond Lake is an exception; we stay overnight to dry out.

We return to the trail near Mount Thielsen, elevation 9,178 feet, one of Oregon's so-called Matterhorn peaks. This massive tower of eroded rock doesn't look like the movie version of a volcano; it looks like a skyscraper that's been hit by a wrecking ball. But in fact, all that cutting and scouring is due to nothing more than wind and water, which has had plenty of time to do its work: Thielsen reached its present approximate height 100,000 years ago, and has been eroding ever since.

Like all of Oregon's Matterhorn peaks (which on our route, include North Sister, Mount Washington, and Three Fingered Jack), Thielsen's sky-piercing profile almost magnetically attracts climbers—and lightning. Its nickname, "lightning rod of the Cascades," gives visitors fair warning. On the summit there's evidence: a peculiar glassy substance called fulgarite is created when repeated electrical charges fuse certain kinds of rocks crystals together. There's a safety lesson here: Outdoor experts frequently suggest that if you're caught high on a ridge in a storm, you should lose elevation—even a few feet will help. If dropping down a couple of yards seems a pathetic solution, consider this: the lightening-fused fulgarite is found only on Thielsen's top five or six feet. Below that, you are (at least, statistically) safer.

The next volcanoes on our route are variations on a theme. All of the others are solo beacons, separated from each other by 40 to 80 miles of lower ridges and lesser peaks. However, the Three Sisters—let's call them Faith, Hope, and Charity, since that's how the early settlers referred to them—are clustered together, along with a few other, lesser relatives.

Such gentle names belie a dysfunctional family of volcanic proportions. We're talking a hotheaded, temperamental group that has spent thousands of years throwing fire at each other and generally misbehaving until the entire lava-littered landscape is a record of family violence.

North Sister, at 10,085 feet, seems to have fared the worst. She's the eldest and most eroded, capped by a Matterhorn-type spire rather than a crater. She doesn't even look like a shadow of her younger self. Middle Sister, at 10,047 feet, is the show-off, a fiery redhead draped in a shining white glacial mantle. But perhaps her glamorous lifestyle is taking its toll, for she, too, is starting to show signs of dissipation. Her red hair, on closer inspection, is made up of crumbling rock rubble, and a huge amphitheater is carved deep in her eastern flank. Of the three, South Sister is the most elegant and best preserved; also, at 10,358 feet, she's the tallest and the only one who has managed to retain her youthful figure. She boasts a circular summit crater, which in the summer collects snowmelt and becomes the highest body of water in Oregon.

The Three Sisters Wilderness is one of the prettiest wildernesses in Oregon, with dozens of alpine lakes and tarns. These volcanoes are also the most protected from human encroachment. Oregon's other major volcanic peaks are all partly on private or multiple-use land; the Three Sisters are entirely surrounded by wilderness. To resupply, we have to drop off the trail and leave the wilderness. But as always in Oregon, there is a lodge nearby.

Deer silhouette, Crater Lake National Park

View of Mount Thielsen from Tipsoo Peak, Mount Thielsen Wilderness

Diamond Peak reflected in Diamond View Lake, Diamond Peak Wilderness

View of Wickiup Plain from South Sister Mountain, Three Sisters Wilderness

Looking north from South Sister Mountain, Three Sisters Wilderness

August 27. Day 114. Mile 1,953. Elk Lake Resort.

We've had several days of on-and-off rain, so we were looking forward to our resupply at Elk Lake Resort. Unfortunately, we became victims of the UPS strike. Pat (our friend who sent us our food resupplies) called Elk Lake Resort a couple of weeks ago and they told her that it was okay to send the package via U.S. mail as long as she sent it in plenty of time. But with the strike, U.S. mail took longer than usual, so our package didn't make it to the lodge; it was still sitting in the post office in Bend, 30 miles away. The proprietors weren't at all helpful; they just said, well you should have sent it UPS, which of course was impossible. So we had to go to Bend. We asked other guests who were heading there to give us a ride. They agreed, even though the owner of the lodge advised them not to take us because "you don't know who they are." Since we had already registered to stay at the lodge (and given identifying information like our address and our credit card number) this seemed not only excessively cautious but plain old mean.

—DAN'S JOURNAL

From Elk Lake, the trail climbs back into the Three Sisters Wilderness up to Koosah Ridge. The ascent seems shocking at first; after the last flat few days, I have forgotten that hiking trails occasionally climb. At the top, we find six other thru-hikers sitting on a rock. It is the largest assembly of thru-hikers we've been with since Kennedy Meadows. Jason, whom we haven't seen since Donner Pass, is there, along with Kirk and Conrad, whom we met for the first time in Castle Crags. There are also three other hikers we've never met before, all going by trail names they adopted on the Appalachian Trail: Squirrel, Knees, and Special K.

Trail names are more a tradition on the AT than on the PCT, but they seem to be catching on out here this year. Jason has picked up the trail name Pokey, which describes his hiking style, if not his actual speed. Over the years, I've heard trail names that echo popular culture (Forest Gimp, Achy-Breaky-Back); names that reflect a hiking style (Slowfoot, Low Gear, Energizer Bunny, Little Engine that Could), favorite animal (in addition to Squirrel, there's a Wolf on the trail), or philosophy (this year, two PCT hikers are confusing everyone by going by the moniker "Let it be.")

Quite possibly, my favorite trail name belongs to a hiker a couple of weeks ahead: Andante. Andante is a musical notation generally translated as "slowly." More accurately, it means "at a walking pace." It's a great name for a music-loving hiker.

I find that often as I walk, my feet march in step to music played in my mind—andante—at a walking pace. Memory music, dredged up from some deep cranial cavity, as though the mountain air has whisked in and scoured out my brain, and now the debris is being expelled out my ears. I hear, in no particular order, folk music from summer camp, love songs from college, classical piano music drummed into my fingers from years of practice. Sometimes I sing, but only when Dan is far ahead or far behind, since he tends to say things like, "Do they have moose in Oregon? I could swear I hear a moose."

The definition of andante, I learn, can be stretched quite a ways if you take "walking pace" literally. On hills, my walking pace is a laborious crawl; Chopin's "Funeral March" will do nicely. On an gentle flat stretch, I stroll easily to the first movement of Beethoven's "Pastoral" symphony. Once, Dave Brubeck's "Take Five" played for a while, and I had to lurch along, fast, in five-quarters time. Often, a tune stays in my head for days on end.

When memory music turns off, mountain music begins.

Water is the melody. High up, the water trickles and drips; lower down, it cascades and roars. Crossing over a creek draining one of the Three Sisters (it is misty; I can't see which one it is), I hear the water echoing against a nearby rock, and I wonder if it always echoes. Will this water sing to this rock for all eternity? Will the rock always answer?

Woodpeckers are the percussion section. You hear them far more often than you see them; they have the habit—like squirrels—of spiraling around to the other side of a tree trunk as you approach. Even if you stop the first minute you hear their telltale hammering, you're unlikely to see them because their sound has a ventriloquist-like quality; it seems to come from nowhere and everywhere. Their calls, however, betray them: they sound like they belong in an Amazonian rain forest.

There are other birdsongs, too: let's make them the wind section. Sweet chickadees singing their three-note song are the flutes. Raucous crows, the trumpets. For our piccolos, we'll choose the tiny peeping of baby grouse that are always scampering in panic along the trail.

I am part of the symphony, too: my breath as I climb, my footsteps on the rocks, the click of my walking sticks.

And, of course, the weather; the ever-changing accompaniment: wind caressing grasses, rustling tree leaves, or gusting, whistling, howling. The muted patter of raindrops on pine duff. The determined, rhythmic splatter of an all-day downpour. Musicians are fond of pointing out that as important as the notes are the silences in between.

At the end of a misty, wet day in the Three Sisters Wilderness, we bed down to the slow movement of the symphony. There is at first the gentle tapping of rain on the tent, the murmur of the nearby stream, the occasional thump as wind knocks down rain that's been collecting on a tree branch. We hear the gentle breath of a chill wind, clearing out the rain.

Then, but for the stream, there is silence.

And in the morning, sun.

When we awaken, the first thing we see is North Sister looming over us. We are camped in an obsidian field, full of nature's jet black, volcanically-fused glass. The Collier Glacier looks like we could reach out and touch it. It is like waking up to find a dinosaur poking its nose inside our tent.

THRU-HIKERS RELAXING AT OVERLOOK IN THREE SISTERS WILDERNESS

But the spectacle is only beginning. North of the Three Sisters, the trail cuts through 65 square miles of lava flows that look like a landscape Steven Spielberg might choose as a stage set for his next dinosaur movie. I'm reminded of those films where pyroclastic flows burn a red path down the sides of active volcanoes in Mexico or Hawaii. Here, it looks like the glowing avalanches simply froze. As far as we can see, dark fields of lava lie over the land like a blanket made of molten rock.

The scene takes me by surprise. I have been in other volcanic landscapes, have climbed volcanoes in other places, but I have never seen anything like this. I've never even seen pictures of anything like this, or heard descriptions. So I walk into this stark and startling place mentally naked. The sight fills a completely empty part of my brain: there's no prototype cluttering up my mind, no lingering picture from a PBS special, no photographs. Even the guidebook authors are uncharacteristically restrained on the subject, telling us only that it is the Cascades' greatest post-Pleistocene outpouring of lava. The surprise, the newness, is unusual in an age where information about everything is instantly accessible. It is an astonishing gift.

To me, this lunar-like landscape (it's not an exaggeration: astronauts actually practiced moon landings here) is one of the most remarkable natural sights I've ever seen, beautiful and terrifying at the same time.

It looks like the earth exploded yesterday.

Actually it didn't: the first major eruptions occurred about 2,900 years ago; later eruptions 1,800 and 1,500 years ago also contributed to the deposits. The mountains responsible for most of these eruptions hardly look up to the task. The towering Sisters now south of us, along with smaller Mount Washington to the north, undoubtedly contributed to the volcanic tempest, but much of the lava flows here come from a handful of puny cinder cones, most notably, Yapoah Crater and Collier Cone.

Only a few hundred feet tall, cinder cones are volcanoes made of pyroclastic lava. The Collier Cone, for instance, was formed about 2,500 years ago during an eruption of one of the Sisters. Pyroclastic material—that is, small fragments of lava that are ejected from the main volcano but solidify before they hit the ground—formed the cinder cone within a matter of weeks.

Dee Wright Observatory and Belknap Crater, Mount Washington Wilderness

View of Mount Washington from unnamed lake, Mount Washington Wilderness

Indian paintbrush, Mount Jefferson Wilderness

Part of the reason for the uneroded appearance of these lava fields is that the lava itself is unusually thick—a product of both volcanic and glacial action. Typically, a glacier scours its way across a landscape, and when it recedes, it leaves a depression. In this case, when the lava was ejected from the cinder cones, it fell on top of the ice, melted it, and then filled the trenches that had held the ice. Had there been no ice-cut depressions for the lava to collect in, the lava probably would have flowed thinner and wider, and might today be much more eroded and hence less dramatic.

Instead, it looks raw. The basalt is course and rough like elephant skin, and it is exactly the same dusky color, midway between gray and brown. You can see that it was once liquid. In some places, the rock is still intact in large chunks the size of—what? What real-world comparisons even have meaning in this elephant-skin landscape where the earth is a mantle of lava, and for perspective, all you can look to are glaciated peaks and the shimmering sky? Are the largest rocks as big as a car? A truck? A house? All of the above, and everything in between.

Regardless of their size, they are crumbling. It's as if the pieces of a three-dimensional jigsaw puzzle are in various stages of being bent and torn away from each other.

The lava flows look lifeless, but they aren't, not entirely. Once in a great while, we pass a scraggly tree that has shown exceptionally bad arboreal judgment and decided to stake a claim. Observing their scraggly independence, their refusal to have anything to do with their fellow trees, their scruffy, trailworn appearance, I'm reminded of hermits and misfits, of people who take to the woods for months at a time (but what am I saying?). The green branches—what there are of them—stand in stark contrast to the dark rocky landscape. Most of the trees die young and small— not, however, before making their tiny contribution to erosion: depositing some organic matter, making fissures that rain and wind will expand into faults, starting the eons-long process of turning rock back to soil. Will the lava field be colonized one tree at a time? It's the typical process of nature, but somehow, I doubt it will happen here. Not if this is all the headway the pioneer trees have been able to make in 2,900 years. Even if the trees do manage to grow, the volcanoes are not extinct. They could erupt again.

Calendars don't mean much to thru-hikers on a day-to-day basis. We need to know what day it is when our world intersects with civilization. For instance, we need to be sure we don't arrive in town on a Saturday afternoon, when the post office will be closed and we can't retrieve our food boxes until Monday. Or if we're going to be in town over a holiday weekend, it makes sense to have reservations in advance if we expect to stay in a motel. The ebb and flow of civilization's cycle occasionally catches us on the trail—on weekends, we'll see more foot traffic than on weekdays.

But we do keep track of time, sort of. It sounds hokey to say we chart our progress by the sun, but it is the sun, rather than the calendar, that gives us the first hint that autumn is in the air. Until now, we've been waking up at 5:30. The early start is a habit left over from our desert days. We kept it up because it allows us to get in big mileage and still take lots of breaks during the day. But now it's too dark to wake up at 5:30; the days are getting shorter. Our wake-up call slides back to 6:00.

I can also tell that it's getting colder because for the first time, I hesitate at the end of the day to jump into whatever body of water happens to be available. Before now, I didn't care if a stream were glacier-fed or if a lake had ice in it; after a hot day of hiking, I was water-bound. But now, the air has acquired a nip, and I find myself wondering if I really do need that bath at the end of the day.

As it so happens, the calendar agrees with the sun: the seasons are indeed changing. It is Labor Day weekend, the end of summer. As we cross the Old Santiam Wagon Road, we see a trailhead packed with dozens of cars, collapsible picnic tables, Coleman lanterns, and dirt bikes. The trail to Three Fingered Jack, a 12-million-year-old plug dome volcano that is the last of the Oregon PCT's sky-piercing Matterhorn peaks, is jam-packed with climbers, day-hikers, and weekend backpackers.

Lightning storm and Mount Jefferson, Mount Jefferson Wilderness

September 1. Day 119. Mile 2,047. Jude Lake.

For me, Labor Day is the real New Year because it means a new school year. Being out here instead of back on the campus puts me in a reflective frame of mind, appreciative of the adventure and the time to have it, but a little bittersweet, because I miss the classroom.

It's also a warning that the hiking season is slowly ending. I am acutely aware how short the window of hiking opportunity is in northern mountains between fall foliage and winter storms. We have 600 miles to go, which is only short if you compare it to the length of the whole PCT. We're not in the homestretch yet.

—DAN'S JOURNAL

Some days, it's hard to believe that weather could ever be a problem—hard to believe in rain or snow, in cold or heat, in whiteouts and blustery winds—when the sun is shining and the sky is friendly and the closest thing to a cloud is a glacier shimmering atop a mountain peak.

At 10,495 feet, Mount Jefferson is the second highest peak in Oregon. Lewis and Clark named the mountain in honor of their presidential patron during their exploration of the Louisiana Territory. On a day like today, it is picture perfect, with a sharp pointy summit and multiple glaciers glistening. (One of them, improbably, drops below treeline).

Clinton Clarke called it:

> *An area unexcelled in the Pacific Northwest as a natural alpine garden sprinkled with lakes and streams, above which rises graceful glacier-hung Mount Jefferson . . . [The] alpine region is a fascinating land of picturesque and friendly beauty, a paradise for the camper and the nature lover.*

Most paradisal of all are the alpine parks, broad sweeps of grasses and flowers that cover the mountain's lower slopes at elevations between 5,500 and 7,000 feet. Jefferson Park is one of them— what scientists call an ecotone, or an edge. These are zones where two ecological communities intersect. In this case, the colliding zones are the forest and the alpine meadow. Characterized by late lying snowpack, the vegetation comprises short-lived wildflowers and grasses, with occasional clumps of trees, depending on the elevation. Late in August, the parks are still bright with snowmelt flowers.

But Mount Jefferson's character is not always so sunny and mild. Streams roar off the glaciers, opaque with the rock flour of glacial wash. Even this late in the season, some of the streams are still frothing, their beds choked with boulders and trees. There is no way to bridge these streams; the bridges would be ripped out with every annual snowmelt. Crossing them requires steady legs and nerves, even after Labor Day.

For us, hiking around Mount Jefferson is almost like hiking in the Sierra, with snowfields to traverse and rushing streams to ford. But ahead is Mount Hood, Oregon's monarch, and here the trail truly feels as though we are taking a path to the sky.

To Native Americans of the region, Hood was Wy'east. According to legend, he was once so tall that when sun shone from the south, his shadow was a whole day's journey to the north. But living in the mountains were evil spirits who threw fire down on the Indians' homes. One day a brave climbed up to end this persecution, which he tried to do by throwing rocks into the homes of the spirits. The spirits threw them back, only now, they were on fire. Seeing that he had caused nothing but destruction, the brave sank to earth and was buried by lava. You can see him, ossified in the north side of the mountain; his profile is a rock formation called the Chief's Face.

Mount Hood, elevation 11,235 feet, is one of the highest of the Cascadian volcanoes (as well as the tallest mountain in Oregon). It is also one of the most visually imposing, by virtue of its location on one of the lowest parts of the Cascade crest. After Fujiyama, it is the second most climbed snow-covered mountain in the world.

It is an active stratovolcano, with a lava flow of up to 8-miles long and 500-feet thick. One of the dominant features of Hood is a 1,700–2,000-year-old debris fan on its southwest slope. A single plug dome (think of it as a pressure valve) exploded, and when it did, the molten matter shot out and melted the ice, which produced mud flows, which in turn produced this debris field. A few hundred

Mountain dogwood, Mount Hood National Forest

feet above the PCT, Crater Rock is what is left of the plug dome. Pools of water near the rock sizzle almost at the boiling point, a demonstration of heated activity below the ground. Could it be that the evil spirits are getting restless?

From the south, the approach to Mount Hood is largely in forest, so views are few and sparse. But once you step on its slopes, it appears as suddenly as an apparition.

Muir, never one to ration his adjectives, becomes positively gushy at the sight:

> *There stood Mount Hood in all the glory of the alpenglow, looming immensely high, beaming with intelligence, and so impressive that one was overawed as if suddenly brought before some superior being newly arrived from the sky . . . The whole mountain appeared as one glorious manifestation of divine power, enthusiastic and benevolent, glowing like a countenance with ineffable repose and beauty, before which we could only gaze in devout and lowly admiration.*

Timberline Lodge, located at the eastern edge of a debris fan, is our goal. The historic mountain lodge was built by the Works Progress Administration during the 1930s; since then, it has been restored and refurbished with careful craftsmanship, from the hand-forged iron banisters to the hand-hewn beams. It is a structure worthy of such a setting.

We are far earlier than check-in time, although with a jacuzzi, a restaurant, a laundromat, a bar, and a store, there's plenty to occupy us until our room is ready.

"Are you hiking the trail?" someone asks, giving us the opportunity to pass time by playing the role of intrepid wilderness adventurers. (That such tough explorers are standing around waiting to get into their rooms in a fairly luxurious lodge is an irony that does not escape us.) We allow as how we are, indeed, hiking the trail.

There is a certain set of questions that follow logically enough. How many pairs of boots have we worn out? (We'll each be on our third pair by the time the trip ends.) Have we seen bears? (Yup.) What do we do when it rains? (Get wet.) How do we resupply? (That's what we're doing right now.) How do we get to take so much time off from work?

It is this last question that I have trouble with, depending on how it's asked. Half of the people are genuinely curious about how you arrange your life so that you can get away for a grand adventure. That's fine—I'm happy to try and explain how we do it. But it seems to me that the other half are looking for excuses; there's a tone that sometimes sounds a lot like, "Must be nice not to have to work." (Sometimes people actually say that.)

To put the record straight, Dan and I both work, and so do most thru-hikers we know. Our careers pay more generously in time than in money. Dan is a college professor, on sabbatical this year. I'm a writer. Neither one of us gets stuck with two-week vacations, so we're lucky in that regard. Then again, we don't get year-end bonuses and stock options. And sometimes, when we are at home, we work for two or three months straight without taking a day off.

Thru-hiking is cheap—it works out to about a $1.50 a mile per person, which is less per day than many people spend living at home. Most of that money is spent on food (an expenditure you'd have at home) and splurges in town like restaurant meals and hotels. Some people spend a lot less. So you don't have to be rich to do it. You just have to want to. All I can say is that there are plenty of all kinds of people of all kinds of professions and jobs and lifestyles on the trail.

The walk from Timberline Lodge to Cascade Locks stays high on the slopes of Mount Hood, following the Timberline Trail around to the mountain's northeast side. It takes us through the Bull Run watershed, where signs warn us to say on the trail. The signs are what's left over from a battle between loggers and environmentalists; and it demonstrates just how complicated the issue of trail routing can get.

The trail here was closed after environmentalists sued the Mount Hood National Forest for permitting logging in the Bull Run watershed, which supplies water to Portland. A judge agreed, but strictly interpreted the 1904 Bull Run Trespass Act, which prohibits all use—and therefore hiking—between Ramona Falls and Interstate 84. The trail was closed from 1973 to 1977; it took an Act

View of Mount Hood from Lolo Pass, Mount Hood National Forest

Punchbowl Falls, Columbia Wilderness

Trees behind waterfall, Columbia Wilderness

Spawning salmon, Eagle Creek, Columbia Wilderness

of Congress, the Bull Run Management Act, to change the boundaries of the watershed and reopen the trails.

September 6. Day 124. Mile 2,144. Eagle Creek.

We left the official PCT near the Indian Springs Trail to drop down into one of my favorite places along the trail (even though it isn't officially on the trail): Eagle Creek. The PCT doesn't follow this spectacular trail, whether because it is overused, or because horses couldn't possible walk on it, I don't know. Like most hikers, we ignored the formalities, and detoured into this beautiful, almost Amazonian canyon where creeks, waterfalls, cascades, little pools, and beautiful forests surround you no matter where you look.

We are camped tonight just 3 miles from the trailhead. Maybe that's why this campsite is such a pigsty. Karen and I spent our first half-hour here picking up trash and burning it. Given the incinerator-sized fire-rings, you'd think people could at least burn their toilet paper, but clearly (disgustingly clearly) that's not the case. Sometimes I get tired of seeing all the little signs, 'pack it in, pack it out,' 'leave only footprints,' and all that. I guess we'll need the signs as long as people think they can trash such a beautiful place as this. Maybe we need $100 fines, too.

—DAN'S JOURNAL

Cascade Locks is our next resupply, our first town since Ashland (unless you count our accidental detour into Bend) and our last stop in Oregon. It's located right next to the Columbia River, which is the only major drainage to cut through the Cascades for 700 miles. On the other side of the bridge, the PCT reaches its lowest point, only 140 feet above sea level.

Also in Cascade Locks are six other hikers we've been leapfrogging with for the past several weeks.

The traveling groups that form among thru-hikers look like they could be used as models of chaos theory. A hiker you met three months ago in California shows up when you're having lunch at a pass in Oregon. Someone you've never even heard of pops out of the woods, and you find yourselves hiking together for 500 miles. Some hikers leave the trail for a few days for a family gathering like a wedding or a graduation, and when they return, the people they knew are 100 miles ahead and there's a whole new group to meet. Power-hikers might do 25- and 30-mile days—followed by three days off in town. A slower hiker doing lower mileage might take less time off—but keep pace with the jackrabbits over the long haul.

In addition to Dan and me, the hikers in town include Kirk, Conrad, Knees, Squirrel, Special K, and Wanchor. Kirk and Conrad are childhood friends. Knees and Squirrel were originally part of a larger group, but the other three have gone on ahead. The two of them plus Special K are all Appalachian Trail veterans, and they're traveling as a threesome, but loosely keeping pace with Kirk and Conrad. The general hiking style of this group seems to be to hike like gang-busters when they're hiking—and in between, to take advantage of every town stop, Taco Bell, hostel, and resupply that they can figure out a way to get to. Wanchor is a solo hiker who compensates for his slow walking pace with dogged determination. He's the only person on the trail who gets up earlier in the morning than Dan and me, and he hardly ever takes more than 24 hours off in town. We first crossed paths with him all the way back at Donner Pass.

The eight of us have different paces, hiking habits, and intended schedules, but we all seem to be ending up at the same places at about the same time. Dan and I are betting we'll be at the Canadian border with at least someone in this group.

Our time in Cascade Locks is not all spent socializing. We have to sort through a mountain of gear we sent ourselves from home. We are now a little ahead of our original schedule. In anticipation of the changing seasons, we shipped ourselves boxes of warmer clothes. But given the warm weather we've had recently, it seems premature to be adding a lot of heavy gear to our packs.

We do take on a few new items: heavier gloves, waterproof over-mitts, better hats—just in case. But most of the gear gets shipped ahead to Snoqualmie Pass, 250 miles north. It is a decision we will have plenty of opportunity—and reason—to second-guess in the days to come.

Mount Adams, Columbia Wilderness

Columbia Gorge, Columbia Wilderness

Bear grass and Surprise Lake with Mount Adams in the distance, Sawtooth Berrypatch area

chapter 5

WASHINGTON: THE WEATHER WILD

Geologist Bates McKee has this to say about Washington weather: "They say you can predict the weather by Mount Rainier. When you can see the mountain, it is going to rain. When you can't see it, it is raining."

We cross into Washington on the Bridge of the Gods. The skies are cloudy but the temperature is warm. The words of Clinton Clarke are whispering in our ears: "Only expert explorers should be on this trail after September 10."

The date is September 9.

The last big push; 500 miles to go.

The Pacific Crest Trail through Washington follows much of the route of the old Cascade Crest Trail, built in the 1930s. In southern Washington, the trail is gentle, rising above treeline into jagged country only once—in the Goat Rocks Wilderness. Like the Oregon PCT, it's a ridge-running route, following the line of volcanic giants northward.

That's the first 250 miles. Then, at Snoqualmie Pass, the trail takes on a distinctly different character as it enters the snaggletoothed North Cascades, where at any day of the year snow can lock a craggy, precipitous landscape in a prison of white.

On September 10, it starts to rain.

Well, okay, we can handle that.

My positive attitude is partly due to the belief that I will find a silver lining in this sky full of clouds. Friends who live hereabouts have assured us that September is the best month for hiking in Washington. They say that the mosquitoes are gone, the huckleberries are ripe, the weather is mild, and it's still the dry season. What Dan and I have yet to figure out is that the local definition of dry season encompasses anything less than a deluge of biblical proportions.

My silver-lined thinking goes something like this: Obviously, it's not going to rain all month. Since I have previously hiked the southern half of Washington, I'd just as soon get the rain over and done with here, where I've already seen the views, and where the terrain is gentle. In return, I expect a fair trade-off: good weather in the more rugged, remote terrain to the north.

If this were a movie instead of a book, the music playing in the background right about now would sound a lot like the theme from *Jaws*.

September 10. Day 129. Mile 2,209. Blue Lake.

This wilderness—the Indian Heaven—is one of my favorite parts of the PCT in Washington, a nice combination of ridgeline trail, lots of good campsites, and pretty country. We arrived here in late afternoon and although we're camped just a couple of hundred feet from the lake, we can't even see it. Tyler, a young thru-hiker we met for the first time today, is camped just down the trail, but tonight's not a night for visiting. Once ensconced in dry clothes in camp, no one is going to brave the elements just to chat. As if to rub in the weather, the guidebook keeps reminding us of the views we're missing: Mount Rainier, Mount Adams, and the gouged eastern flank of decapitated Mount St. Helens.

—DAN'S JOURNAL

Local Indian myths differ in their detail, but the gist is good for a legend in any culture.

Mount St. Helens is a fair maiden named La-wa-la-clough. The beautiful newcomer to the neighborhood catches the eye of local boys Pahto (Mount Adams) and Wy'east (Mount Hood). The maiden prefers broad shouldered, massive, manly Pahto. Wy'east does the predictable thing and flies into a rage, striking Pahto and flattening his head. Pahto is defeated. In humiliation he keeps his head down forever and never smokes again.

The legend leaves unanswered questions about La-wa-la-clough, the comely maiden. Was she disappointed that Pahto didn't better rise to the occasion, perhaps by hurling fire or spewing rocks? Is that why she became shriller and shriller, throwing so many temper tantrums that the local Klickitat people started calling her "fire mountain?"

Whatever the reason, her tragic end is clear: finally, in a volcanic act of suicide, she blew her top.

Beginning on May 18, 1980, Mount St. Helens started erupting and, by the time she was finished, 1,300 feet of the formerly 9,677-foot peak were blown to smithereens.

The explosion was equivalent to 30 million tons of TNT, produced a lava flow 4 miles long, melted the upper 45 feet of a glacier, killed 57 people, felled trees on more than 100,000 acres, and spewed ash that circled the globe.

The PCT leads us right around the flank of Mount Adams, only 30 miles from the scarred and battered body of his once-beloved beauty. Some of her ash lies on his flanks; after the Mount St. Helens explosion, the PCT here was so deeply covered in ash that it was unhikeable.

For this part of our journey, we're traveling in the literary company of Supreme Court Justice William O. Douglas, a lifelong walker whose backpacking accomplishments included hiking the entire Appalachian Trail. Published in 1960, Douglas's *My Wilderness*, sounds a tone that matches both the reverence and the passion of John Muir:

> *I learned . . . an important lesson in ecology . . . that wilderness areas are essential to our long-term welfare and well-being as a nation . . . Will the next generation ever have the chance to experience the same feeling of serenity and composure that comes when man faces the wilderness alone?*

Like Muir, Douglas writes about experiences so close to our own that it seems that we must have missed crossing paths with each other by minutes, not decades. Hiking around Mount Adams, we have to rely on Douglas to describe the views for us. As it turns out, old Pahto's bowed head is not always easy to see:

> *I may not see it for hours on end as I travel this mountain area, for the trail is usually beneath a ridge. Yet when I travel there, I almost always feel the presence of the mountain. I am filled with the expectancy of seeing it from every height of land, at every opening of a canyon. And the sight of its black basalt cliffs crowned with white snow, both set against a blue sky, is enough to make a man stop in wonderment.*

With a misty curtain of fog obscuring our view, we have to settle for feeling the presence of the mountain. That presence is cold and wet.

It's very different weather than anything we've had before. Rain in August in Oregon never lasted all day and all night and on into the next day. It never prevented us from eating lunch or having a snack. The few times we made camp in the rain, we awoke to sunny skies.

Now we've turned the corner from summer into fall. Temperatures are lower, the rain is colder, and it does last all day. Here in the hypothermia zone, the rules have changed, and we have to change with them.

Rule number one: We can't let ourselves get cold. This means paying attention to how we feel, to how dry our clothing is, to how many layers we are wearing. Rule number two is a corollary of rule number one: If stopping means getting cold, we can't stop. We need to choose a pace that is sustainable all day, a pace that will keep us warm without making us sweat from over-exertion. Rule number three: We need to keep our energy up. Since we can't sit around taking long lunch breaks, this means grabbing a quick bite on the fly, maybe huddled under a tree, maybe wolfing down a snack as we walk.

One thing we notice: rainy weather encourages bigger mileage. There are no roses to slow down and smell. Walking is the only thing that keeps us warm, so we walk. And then walk some more.

September 13. Day 131. Mile 2,273. Sheep Lake.

By the time we got to camp last night, I was so tired and wet I didn't even finish writing my journal notes. We broke camp in the rain, walked 22 miles in the rain, made camp in the rain, cooked in the rain, and slept in the rain. It is like living in a shower.

But this morning, we awoke to a promise of sunshine, and we actually broke camp in dry weather. A couple of miles down the trail, we caught up with Wanchor, who was sitting at a road crossing trying to decide whether or not to quit the hike. We are now only 385 miles from the Canadian border. Wanchor hates hiking in the rain. So far he's managed to avoid it; he just stays in his tent, or in town, until the weather clears. That worked fine in Oregon, but here it would mean staying in his tent for days on end or maybe forever. We left him with a few encouraging words and told him where we would be tonight so he could camp with us if he wanted company, but so far he hasn't shown up. Maybe he did get off after all. It's too bad, because today the weather was okay, with intermittent views of Adams and Rainier. It didn't actually start raining again until just as we reached camp. This was our first almost dry day since Cascade Locks.

—Dan's journal

The next morning, it is still dark when Dan nudges me.

"Are you awake?"

"I am now," I say grumpily.

"I've been thinking about something." he says.

I am not a gracious waker-upper. I don't care what anyone is thinking about at 5:30 in the morning in the dark in the rain. Especially in the rain.

Hikers like to say how soothing the pitter-patter of raindrops is on a nylon tent, how snug it feels to be inside, how the sound lulls you to sleep.

I am sick of raindrops and their cursed sound.

I roll over and burrow deeper inside my sleeping bag. But when Dan has something on his mind, he's not easy to deter.

"I've been thinking maybe we shouldn't go up there," he says.

Up there is the Goat Rocks Wilderness, the highest, most exposed alpine landscape on southern Washington's PCT. Sacred to the Yakima Indians, this eroded remains of an old volcano was said to be home of *La-kin-nie*, the god of goats. I don't know about *La-kin-nie*, but Dan and I have seen plenty of his subjects up there on previous trips. It's a spectacular place.

Columbia tiger lily, Sawtooth Berrypatch area

View of Mount Rainier from Goat Rocks Wilderness

Lupine with Mount Rainier in the distance, Mount Rainier National Park

"Goat Rocks seem holy to me—of this earth and yet apart from it," wrote Douglas. "They are sanctuaries but on such a vast scale that he who approaches them from the south is certain to feel humble and reverent."

Well, yes, but that assumes that you can see them.

We lie in our tent waiting for the sun to come out. It doesn't.

Dan studies the map. He's concerned about the obstacles up high: a glacier to cross, followed by 2 miles atop an exposed knife-edge ridge, followed by an equally exposed descent. From here to White Pass, it's 25 miles, and much of the traverse is above treeline in wilderness. There are no alternate routes that circumvent the high ridges, and once you are up there, the only way to get out is to continue up and over.

There's no good way to avoid the traverse. We could backtrack, I suppose, or drop off the trail and walk until we crossed a road, but that would take us many miles in the wrong direction. Once out of the wilderness, we'd be so far off-route that we'd have to hitchhike on backwoods roads that most likely wouldn't have any traffic.

"I want to try to go up," I say. This is consistent. Dan is stronger than I am, but in conditions that skirt the margins of safety, he's also more conservative. Partly, I think it's because he's worried that I'll overestimate my strength, which I have been known to do.

But that's not the case this time.

Besides, this is a thru-hike. We're supposed to hike through things, not around them.

(And here, incidentally, is the validation of the slippery slope theory. Remember Yosemite? If we had hitchhiked around the difficulties back then, wouldn't it be just that tiny bit easier to drop off the trail to a road and hitchhike here? We stuck it out through Yosemite; we can do this, too.)

The sky is not encouraging. The air is filled with a misty drizzle that is less like rain than like wet air. Once in awhile, a cloud breaks apart, but before we even have time to look for the blue, a new cloud forms and takes its place. Up we go, stopping only to add layers of clothing. With each 100 feet we gain, the temperature drops a smidgen, and the wind seems meaner. But when we pass the last side trail—our last chance to bail out—we pause for only a second.

"You okay with this?" I ask Dan, and he nods.

Up and up. Amazing how much difference a few hundred feet can make. The trees shrink into twisted little dwarfs. Junipers hug the earth. You have to admire them, staking their ground so stubbornly. The wind that bent them whips across our faces. The rain turns to sleet.

We step into the clouds at the snow line, where late-lingering snowfields block our path. Stone cairns point the way, but once we are enveloped by the fog, there is no visibility. Nor are there footprints to follow across the snow; they have been erased by the rain and sleet that has been falling for the last few days.

William O. Douglas:

I have never felt the thrill of wind as keenly as I have here…A blistering wind roars across [the Goat Rocks]. It comes with great gusto from the west. It is so strong that voices seem swept away almost before the words are uttered.

As usual, it's like he's right here with us. The wind snatches our voices out of our throats and steals them away. We need our voices, or a whistle. Sound is a lifeline that connects us to each other. As we stand in the middle of a snowfield, out of sight of the last cairn, not yet able to see the next one, we are lost in a sea of snow and fog.

"Uphill," Dan shouts. "Stay up!"

I try to remember why I thought the trail led down, but I'm all turned around now. I am afraid to let Dan go beyond the sound of my voice, but I'm also afraid to venture any farther away from the last place I knew the trail to be. The guidebook maps are inadequate for these conditions, with print that is too small to read and out-of-date information.

But we can't just stand here and wait for the fog to break. The fog is not going to break.

Keep moving, I think. Have to move. When in doubt, go up. Always go up.

"Over here!"

CAMPSITE IN GOAT ROCKS WILDERNESS

Above me, Dan has found some footprints, which lead to a trail, which splits in two. Now we know where we are. We have to decide: Do we go up, over the wind-sheared shoulder of Old Snowy Mountain? Or do we stay low and cross the upper slopes of the Packwood Glacier?

Originally, we intended to take the high route. In good weather, the scramble to the 7,930-foot summit offers a panoramic view. Today it would be like looking through a milk bottle. Also, the wind will become fiercer on the mountain's higher slopes. Already we can barely keep our footing under the assault of the strong, unpredictable gusts.

So we choose the lower path. As far as glaciers go, this is a fairly safe one to cross. There are no crevasses, no seracs, no ice falls, no fantastic ice sculptures. But a glacier is still a glacier, and as gentle as its slope might be, it's steep enough to send you on a long downhill slide if you fall. I am acutely aware that we have long since sent our ice axes home.

The wind hurls itself at us in impetuous gusts. The footing is slippery from rain and sleet. Below me, the slope descends into endless fog. Fortunately, we have trekking poles—two each—so I concentrate on having three points on the snow at all times: one foot and two walking sticks, or two feet and one stick. When the wind gusts, I freeze in place, and try to press my weight into the mountain. The hood of my rain gear crackles and snaps around my face like a torn sail. The noise of the wind fills my universe, which has shrunk to pure, immediate sensation. Each step takes an eternity.

When the glacier ends, the knife-edge ridge begins.

"The trail is only a few feet wide; the drop-off on each side is so great that some people get vertigo," says Douglas. Like Muir, he seems to embrace conditions like these. "It is indeed like walking the cornice of the Empire State Building."

Okay, well here's a silver lining for these clouds: Since my view of the drop-off is blocked by the fog, it can't trigger my acrophobia.

The trail itself is most often not on the actual crest of the knife edge, but just a few feet to one side or the other of it. On the windward side we lurch and flail about like marionettes in the hands of rambunctious toddlers. When we cross to the leeward side, the wind simply stops. One second it roars; the next it's absolutely silent. It's like turning off the stereo just when the cannons are blasting away in Tchaikovsky's "1812 Overture."

Finally we turn leeward and leave the crest. It is a much longer descent that I remember. We drop below the clouds and visibility returns: we see glaciated gray basins, gray crumbled rock, gray clouds above, gray valley below. Far away and endlessly down, there is green.

Down and down. It has been hours since we started walking, but still we cannot stop. There is no shelter and no protection; needlelike shards of rain sting my skin with a force that seems intentional.

I am tired, wired, drunk on adrenaline. Every nerve is exposed and agitated. There is no longer any barrier between me and the weather. I am wind and rain and cold.

An eternity passes.

Finally—we have been walking without rest for five and a half hours—the rain thins to a half-hearted misty drizzle. A clump of trees offers some protection. Quickly, we boil up water for tea. The warmth of the hot liquid feels almost exotic, but we can't linger in luxury; the weather is still too cold, too wet. Fifteen minutes later, we are walking again. By the time we pull into camp, we have been walking for 19.6 miles and 11 hours; we have taken exactly one 15-minute break.

September 14. Day 132. Mile 2,288. Ridge near Tieton Pass.

People who have been in a war often come home with irreconcilable emotions: they remember the horror of it, but they also remember the intensity of a moment-to-moment, life-and-death existence. Some say that they never felt as alive.

You can't compare backpacking to war. Nor would I call today horrible (wet, cold, long, tiring, potentially hypothermic, slightly dangerous, yes; but all of that doesn't add up to horrible). Still, there was a comparable sort of intensity. I wouldn't want an endless succession of days like this, but to tell the truth, we're both feeling a little high right now.

—DAN'S JOURNAL

Wildflowers at Chinook Pass, Mount Rainier National Park

Descending from the high ridges down into White Pass is like returning from a strange netherworld where humans were never meant to go. The woods feel comforting and friendly. The same old rain is falling, but it's just rain now; it's no longer an evil force acting with malevolent intent.

As we walk along the road that crosses the pass, people peer at us from the cocoon of their cars, insulated and protected by windshield wipers and heaters and defrosters and glass.

Little things seem extraordinary, like the fact that the store at the pass boasts an espresso bar. Even the heat in the store seems exotic.

To further test our sense of the ridiculous, a young man from a local television station shows up to interview us for a story he's doing about the PCT. Would we mind, he asks, going back outside to the trail so he can get some action footage of us slogging through puddles in the rain?

After the interview, we ask the reporter whether he has heard a weather forecast, and he smiles. I know that smile; it's the look you get anytime you ask about the local bugaboo. You see it in Tennessee when talk turns to rattlesnakes, or in Montana when you ask about grizzly bears, or Maine when you ask about black flies.

"Oh, when it gets like this, you can forget about seeing the sun for a week," he says cheerfully.

The rest of our day in White Pass is spent drying out. There are eight of us hikers holed up here in motel rooms, all hoping that the dire forecasts people seem to insist on sharing with us are just a lot of local ballyhoo. But it's still raining when we head out into the next wilderness, which, I am delighted to learn, is named after William O. Douglas.

It's ridiculous weather for hiking, but it's not like we have a choice. We can't afford the time to sit around waiting for the sun. The later in the season it gets, the worse it's going to be, because in addition to rain, we now have to start thinking about snow. Only two weeks ago, the snow line was up somewhere around 11,000 feet; now it's all the way down to 6,500 feet. That means the rain down here is snow back up in the Goat Rocks.

Kirk, who has a radio, occasionally updates us on the forecasts, which alternate between "rain followed by showers" and "showers followed by rain." I don't know whether it's a sign of mental health or a sign of insanity that we all think that this is funny.

So we pull out the old positive attitudes and put on a bit of false bravado, and we walk. It's still raining.

If you've ever owned a lemon of a car, you know how optimism can lead to despair. The next repair will fix the problem. Only a hundred dollars more. Just another gasket to replace and she'll be purring like a cat.

We tell ourselves that if we made it through the Goat Rocks, we can make it through anything. We take heart that it is only drizzling, that it's not too cold, that the trail stays below treeline, that climbing will keep us warm. We convince ourselves that sooner or later the sky has to run out of rain.

But it doesn't. The day wears on; it wears us down. The trail is underwater. Our clothing is wet, our boots are sponges. Dan and I walk and eat our lunch at the same time, trying to keep our crackers dry in zip lock bags. They turn to soggy wads before we can even get them from hand to mouth. And worst of all, after 2,300 miles on the trail, I am developing blisters on my toes from the nonstop combination of wet feet, wet socks, and wet boots slogging through a wet trail.

Dusk finds the eight of us split up according to walking pace. Dan and I are alone on a ridge where the few flat spots are all several inches under water. Finally, we find a place that's big enough for the tent, flat enough to sleep on, and dry enough that we won't wake up doing the breast stroke. The other camping necessity—a water source—is, to say the least, not a problem. A nearby puddle has enough water for an entire scout troop; all we have to do is fill the water bag using our pot as a scoop.

Of course, this is the night our stove decides to stop working.

I have to say that in recent years, Dan and I have become star-crossed when it comes to stoves. For years, I regarded stoves with the same sort of superstitious dread with which I regard car engines and home furnaces. My relation to them involved chanting "Please work, please work, please, please, please." And for the most part, they did. Then I started writing books about backpacking, and it occurred to me that if I was going to assume the voice of authority, I should know something

Old-growth forest along the Trail, Alpine Lakes Wilderness

Waptus Lake in morning light, Alpine Lakes Wilderness

about stoves. So I read the instruction manuals. I begged lessons from the sales reps. I hounded more knowledgeable hiking pals to share their secrets. Knowledge is power, right? Or maybe it is the forbidden fruit. Because the god of stoves, who used to answer my prayers, now ignores them, and I find myself frequently tinkering with the blasted things—always, of course, on rainy nights when my fingers are so cold and wet that they feel like wooden sticks attached to my hands.

The problem this time is easy enough to figure out and fix (it involves a malfunctioning cleaning needle that is supposed to keep the jet through which the gas flows open). But it takes several attempts and a lot of swearing before I get it right.

The next morning when we wake up, it is still raining, the stove is still sputtering and something in both of us, simply, snaps.

This is the bad part. I guess it would be unreasonable to expect two people to be able to hike through all the challenges Dan and I have faced without at least one big blowout. Our fellow hikers have been sharing tales of little incompatibilities: one partner wants to go into town, one wants to walk on. Both think they are doing all the compromising. Etcetera. As tempted as you might be to declare, "Well, I'll just pack up my stuff and meet you later," you can't. There is no "my" stuff; there is only "our" stuff. Hiking partners (not to mention hiking partners who are also married couples) have to agree on everything, and this morning, Dan and I can manage to agree on nothing. Our disagreement expands to fill our universe. We argue about what time to get up, how to pack up so our gear doesn't get wetter, whether to try to cook when the stove starts to sputter, what's wrong with the stove, whether to consider bailing out for a couple of days, and whether to just quit the whole damn trip this exact minute.

It is not our finest hour on the trail.

A toilet saves the day.

After we've cooled our heels and our tempers—which takes about half a day—we reach Chinook Pass, on the border of Rainier National Park. Usually, this road is full of cars, but today it's closed for repairs just east of the pass. You can only drive up here from the western side, and the only reason to do that would be for sightseeing or for hiking, neither of which are going to big draws on a day like this. We never did resolve the issue of whether to hitchhike out; the lack of traffic makes the decision for us.

As we approach the vault-like building that houses the restrooms, I am hoping that some hyperefficient ranger hasn't locked them for the season. But we're in luck: the door is unlocked. Shelter, at last!

Inside, it's like stepping into a sensory deprivation chamber. I, for one, am delighted to have my senses deprived of gusting wind and dripping rain. Something so simple as being able to open our packs without getting all our gear wet seems like the height of luxury. So does eating our crackers before the rain turns them into soggy lumps. Or putting on extra layers of clothing without the complex choreography needed to keep everything dry in the rain.

I would happily sleep in the restroom, but it's still early in the day and our guidebook tells us that 8 miles ahead, we will pass a side trail to one of the few shelters on or near the PCT.

Dan and I do not regard this information as a promise, only a possibility. Our guidebook is out of date. The last shelter it told us about had deteriorated into a pile of rocks. The policy in wilderness areas is to let old structures fall to the ground. When we arrive at the turnoff that leads to the shelter, I look at my watch so I can measure off the half-mile to where the lean-to is supposed to be. Assuming that we are doing our usual 3-mile-an-hour downhill pace, it will take us 10 minutes to get there.

I have never wanted anything more in my entire hiking life than to see the roof of that lean-to. I don't care what kind of condition it's in. Even a falling-down shack would give us somewhere to sort out our gear and cook out of the rain. If there are holes in the roof, we can cover them with our ground cloth. I'm willing to settle for anything.

After only five minutes of walking, I spot a roof. Coming closer, I see that it is reasonably intact. The walls are punctured with holes, but there's no question that the shelter is usable. Under other circumstances, you might question the aesthetics of this admittedly ugly, run-down, building. You might turn up your nose and pitch your tent outside. I've heard land managers (and some hikers) say that lean-tos don't belong

Mountain blueberries in Henry M. Jackson Wilderness

in wilderness areas, that they draw crowds, that they are antithetical to the wilderness experience, that people who hike in these areas should be prepared for the conditions. If you want lean-tos, go hike on the wussy Appalachian Trail. And so on.

My personal opinion is that this discussion should be forbidden in bars, in conference rooms, and on sunny days. If you want to argue about whether shelters belong in the wilderness, you should go to the wilderness. Moreover, you should go there when the week-long forecast is for rain followed by showers, when the wind is high and the temperatures are low, and you should stay there for a while. A week, I think, will do. If you come out of that still advocating the elimination of all shelters—if you arrive at Big Crow Basin on a day like today, after a yesterday like yesterday, after a week like last week, and you turn up your nose at the shelter and pitch your tent in the muddy field—well, I take my hat off to you.

In my case, there is no doubt. It takes me a nanosecond to get myself and gear under that roof. When I see that the dirt floor is actually dry and that someone has left a pile of firewood, I feel hot water running down my cheeks. It isn't rain.

September 17. Day 135. Mile 2,338. Big Crow Basin Shelter.

A day that began terribly ended beautifully.

On a practical note, we're happy to see that our equipment has weathered the last two days much better than we expected. The worst casualties are our boots, which are torched, and the clothes we've been walking in all day, which are damp. Our hats and gloves are soaked, but they'll dry out. The things that really need to dry still are our nighttime warm clothes and our sleeping bags. Two pieces of gear have out-performed themselves: Our old Northface Tadpole tent proved tight as a drum, and our Outdoor Research waterproof stuff-sacks kept our sleeping bags nearly bone dry.

We didn't even have to use the balky stove tonight; I made a fire with the shelter's stash of dry wood. Now, we're warm and mostly dry; we've eaten and we have shelter. Outside, the field is full of snow, which started falling as soon as the nighttime temperatures dropped below freezing. But the snowfall has stopped now, and the clouds are traveling fast and breaking up. Every once in a while, the full moon shines over the snowy field.

—Dan's Journal

Waptus Lake in evening light, Alpine Lakes Wilderness

Snoqualmie Pass is our next resupply, about 60 miles away. For most of these miles, the trail passes through lumbering operations.

In the early days of the PCT, hiking enthusiasts floated a proposal to surround the trail with a 10-mile-wide corridor of wilderness. The purpose of a protective corridor is obvious: A hiking trail is only as good as the land it traverses. But a 10-mile-wide corridor was an almost naively ambitious idea. In comparison, the corridor that is supposed to surround the PCT's older sibling, the Appalachian Trail, is only 1,000-feet wide. Even that modest goal has proved gargantuan in the face of out-of-control development and escalating eastern property values.

On the PCT, the idea of a protective corridor fizzled in the face of reality. Getting the trail finished was ambitious enough, let alone protecting land on either side of it. Besides, the PCT isn't as threatened as the AT: a higher percentage of the PCT is on public land, which offers a measure of protection. And population density near the PCT, along with the concomitant pressures of development and commercial land use, is much lower than it is in the East.

Where the PCT does pass through private property, no attempt has been made to regulate, control, or influence land use. Easements granted to the trail simply ensure the right of passage. If the landowner wants to clearcut, hikers will just have to hike through a clearcut. There is also some clearcutting on public lands near the trail. Forest Service brochures rather disingenuously put a public relations spin on the issue of multiple-use detritus: they tell us that the trail gives hikers not only the opportunity to walk through pristine wilderness, but also the chance to see and appreciate how our public lands are used. They point out that such uses are approved by the trail's management plan, as if that should make a difference.

The last time I walked this stretch of trail, it made me sick. It looks like a crazy quilt thrown upon the hillsides. Patches of forest alternate with patches of clearcut. You step out of cool shady forest and cross a battle line into devastation. Depending on how long ago the parcel was clearcut, it might be a mess of snag and lumber debris, or perhaps a field full of huckleberry bushes, or maybe a plantation of unnatural-looking, even-aged, second-growth timber. The footway is eroded, uneven, and difficult to walk on. In summer, stepping into a clearcut is like stepping into an oven; the temperature is a good 20 degrees higher than it is in the surrounding forest. In rainy fall, it is like diving into a swimming pool, because rain-drenched shoulder-high huckleberry bushes overgrow the trail. From the clearcut, the next island of forest becomes your goal, as if you were a shipwreck survivor swimming to shore. But when you reach the patch of forest, you see a lot number nailed to a tree, reminding you that this little island of forest is no more than a future clearcut.

As far as following the official trail through here is concerned, I have only one thing to say: Been there, done that, not gonna do it again.

September 20. Day 138. Mile 2,396. Snoqualmie Pass.

We found an alternate route between Tacoma Pass and Snoqualmie Pass that took us along a series of roads but out of the clearcuts. I can't stand looking at the scarred hillsides. It reminds me of when some lunatic took a chisel to the face of the "Pieta."

Our road walk wasn't any shorter than the trail, and it didn't involve any less climbing; it just got us out of the destruction. And—an added bonus—the weather was good. After a slight sprinkle in the morning, the skies cleared. We got great views of Rainier behind us, poking up through a misty sea of cotton-candy clouds. Ahead of us, we got our first views of the snow-covered North Cascades. The prospect of climbing up into that fierce-looking country in the kind of weather we've been having lately is, frankly, terrifying.

—DAN'S JOURNAL

Glacier Lake and distant Glacier Peak, Alpine Lakes Wilderness

Lake Valhalla and Mount Lichtenberg, Henry M. Jackson Wilderness

At 3,127 feet, Snoqualmie Pass is the lowest and most heavily traveled pass across Washington's Cascades. It's got a small ski area; other than that, I don't know what its attraction is for tourists, but it must have one. At least 100 cars are parked in the lot outside the motel, and there's an endless stream of people coming and going; I have no idea to and from what. When we ask about a room, the manager says that he doesn't know whether he has any; we will have to wait while he figures it out.

Our stop here is necessary for several reasons, not the least of which is our sanity. We need to dry out and take a good hard look at our gear. The much-needed boxes of warm clothes we shipped ahead from Cascade Locks should be waiting for us at the post office. We're also expecting a new pair of boots for Dan (his third pair of the trip), since pair number two limped into the pass held together with duct tape and seam-sealer compound. And we've decided to add a couple of other pieces of equipment: a different stove, since we're sick of fussing with our sputtering MSR, a tarp—not instead of our tent, but in addition to it—so we can rig up a cooking and gear-sorting area on rainy nights.

While we're waiting for the motel manager to count rooms, we go over to the post office, which occupies a corner of the general store. The post office is closed, but if we're willing to wait until business quiets down the proprietress will get our boxes for us. So we wait, and wait, while people stream in and out, purchasing plastic logging trucks and rubber eagles and postcards. This many people in this small a space is overwhelming. My reaction—anxiety, nerves, and disorientation—makes me wonder if I'll be able to stand in line at a New York deli ever again.

Finally, we get our boxes—and our motel room—and we spend the day drying out. Kirk, Conrad, Knees, Squirrel, and Special K come in after us. We thought they were ahead, but the weather got to them, too; they dropped behind by hitching a ride out of Chinook Pass (the pass where Dan and I huddled in the toilet facility). Tyler, however, has gone on. Nobody has heard anything about Wanchor.

One thing we do hear: A good weather report. Four days of good weather, to be precise. So when we head out into the North Cascades, the last major chunk of the Pacific Crest Trail, we tackle the 2,800-foot climb with big smiles.

William O. Douglas:

> *The mountains of the Pacific Northwest are tangled, wild, remote, and high. They have the roar of torrents and avalanches in their throats . . . Snowcapped peaks with aprons of eternal glaciers command the skyline . . . There are no slow-moving, sluggish rivers in these mountains. The streams run clear, cold, and fast. There are remote valleys and canyons where man has never been. The meadows and lakes are not placid idyllic spots. The sternness of the mountains has been imparted to them . . . Trails may climb 4,000 feet or more in 2 miles. In 20 miles of travel one may gain, then lose, then gain and lose once more, several thousand feet of elevation.*

The profile map in our data book graphically represents the climbs and descents. It looks like the EEG of someone on crack cocaine. To attach facts to hyperbole: In the next four days, we will climb and descend a total of 12,600 feet in 75 miles.

This is unusual for the PCT. The North Cascades are serrated mountains, with steep gorges and deep valleys. It's a glacial landscape of cirques, vertical headwalls, and moraines. Field geologist Stephen Harris says, "Seemingly locked in a contemporary ice age, this remote and stormy terrain is one of the last true wilderness areas in the United States."

Added to that, our elevations are beginning to increase. Once we climb out of Snoqualmie Pass, we'll be up around 5,000 feet; farther north, we'll go all the way back to 7,000 feet. Consider, also, that this far north, the treeline is down around 5,200 feet. This late in the season, the snow line is dropping, too.

Sauk River drainage, Glacier Peak Wilderness

But for the moment, who cares? Finally, we have a forecast to celebrate: four days of sun. One thing that the weather has done is blast away every concern I had about the steep climbs ahead. If we're going to have dry weather, I intend to celebrate; I don't care how tough the trail is.

After the two weeks of wet weather, it is sheer luxury to feel the sun on my skin. The trail through the Alpine Lakes Wilderness lives up to its name and its reputation. The designation of this area as wilderness precipitated a bitter fight in the 1970s. Ironically, now that mining and logging have been curtailed, too much backcountry use threatens the area's pristine quality. Alpine Lakes is under siege from the double threat of accessibility (it's right off of I-90) and proximity (it's a short drive from the burgeoning Seattle metropolitan area). I have to say that for a weekday in September, it seems pretty crowded to us. Maybe that's just because every cabin-fevered Washingtonian is seizing the moment to take advantage of the good weather forecast.

For this section, we're planning high mileage (my preference, not Dan's). Dan wants to try to focus on enjoying each one of the days left rather than being preoccupied with getting to Canada. I want to do the 75 miles in four days because I'm concerned about the weather.

Up and down and up and down; we haven't done this kind of hiking since the High Sierra. But it's easier now, after more than 2,000 miles on the trail. Or maybe I'm just not paying attention to the climbs because there's so much to see. Colors, for one thing. I haven't seen colors in days, and now there are greens and yellows and the orange-red of the huckleberry bushes—not to mention the purple-black huckleberries themselves. And there are mountains everywhere, tightly serrated, fiercely jagged peaks jutting into blue sky. Blue—another color I haven't seen lately.

September 25. Day 143. Mile 2,471. Skykomish.

Four days of glory, then the minute we got to Stevens Pass and started to hitchhike to our resupply, it started to rain. What timing! Still, it took an hour—and 200 cars passing us— before someone picked us up. I guess you can't blame people for not stopping, but it's a terribly vulnerable feeling to be stuck needing a ride and all you can do is smile and stick

Black bear in Glacier Peak Wilderness

out your thumb and hope. Kirk and Conrad, then Squirrel and Knees, came down after us, with hitching stories of their own. Kirk and Conrad got picked up by a certifiable lunatic. Knees, frustrated by the stream of cars that were passing by, made an obscene gesture at a car, which then turned around and came back. The driver said, "You must really need a ride if you did that"—and then drove them into town! Now that's a novel hitching strategy!

People news: We just met Dave, a thru-hiker who goes by the trail name Breaking Wind. (People actually call him that.) We've been hearing about him for hundreds of miles, but this is the first time we've met. And Wanchor is still on the trail. After getting lost in the Goat Rocks, he bushwhacked out and got a ride with some Indians from the Yakima Reservation. He got back on the trail a day later, and is now in town with us.

—DAN'S JOURNAL

We have set a date to arrive at Manning Park: October 9. We have 14 days left. It's raining now, and the forecast is for more of the same. Dan and I are armed for the coming battle with the new tarp and the new stove. Our mood is resolute. We plan to take six days to get to Stehekin, the last resupply on the entire trip. The rest of the hikers are planning to do it in five.

The first two days are mostly wet, although not constantly. The first night we make camp in a drenched meadow that is almost ghostly in the misty half-light of falling dusk. Trees emerge from the gloom and fade back into it.

The next day is more of the same, neither pleasant nor unpleasant, only wet. In the morning we pack up a wet tent and a wet tarp and put on our wet clothes and walk through the wet forest. A month ago, this would have been hardship. Now it is merely soggy routine.

Dusk finds us at Lake Sally Ann, a tiny tarn just at treeline, and a popular camping spot, judging from the obviously oft-used campsites. Today, it's just us thru-hikers. As the temperature drops, we notice that the clouds are breaking apart, letting in slivers of sunlight, glimmers of hope.

The hike tomorrow is not just any ordinary section of the PCT. Tomorrow's walk is an above-treeline traverse of one of the trail's legendary beauty spots. If we could have but a single day of good weather in the entire state of Washington, tomorrow is the day I would have chosen. I haven't been counting on it— nor even daring to hope. After all, it's not like my weather preferences have exactly been granted in the last month or so.

Miraculously, the wind stays dry and the temperature stays low. Visibility increases. When I wake up at night, the stars are twinkling a promise. In the morning, I can feel that a high-pressure front has rolled in; even before I stick my head out of the tent, I sense that the sky is clear.

It's an unbelievable gift.

Today is a reward for all of our soggy days, made more precious because we have earned it. Above the 6,500-foot elevation, new snow sparkles on the surrounding peaks. Our trail for the first half of the day bounces between 5,000 and 6,500 feet; then it dives down to 3,700 feet. Mostly, we will be above treeline.

We can see all the way back to Rainier. The giant mountain looms over the landscape like an oversized dinosaur in a kiddie cartoon. It seems even larger from far away than it did up close; completely, ridiculously out of proportion to the terrain. At 14,410 feet, Rainier towers over the craggy North Cascades as though they were foothills. You could take a photograph and subtitle it, "The mountain that ate the Northwest."

It could, too. Twenty-five hundred years ago, it erupted and dumped so much debris that it changed the shape of the Puget Sound coastline. Indians called Rainier the "mountain that is god." European-Americans, as usual, named it after some official, in this case a British admiral.

The trail winds its way to White Pass. More and more rows of white peaks come into view. The lower hills are covered with patches of color: golden grasses, green trees, and everywhere the flaming orange-red understory of huckleberry bushes. The sky is brilliant. By the time we reach Red Pass, Dan has shot two-and-a-half rolls of film.

Mica Lake with Dome Peak in the distance, Glacier Peak Wilderness

Creeklet near Suiattle River, Glacier Peak Wilderness

Image Lake and Glacier Peak, Glacier Peak Wilderness

And now, Glacier Peak is the mountain that fills the sky. It is a very different mountain than any we have yet circumambulated. It is not as big as Rainier, but where Rainier seems a solid monarch, Glacier Peak has a raw, violent quality.

From Red Pass, we go down into the canyon of the White Chuck River—Chuck is the Chinook word for water; white refers to the glacial flour that makes the water look opaque as milk. The canyon is a monochromatic palette of gray and white rock and snow.

The trail drops into forest that gets denser and darker as we descend. Our trail is a transition through life zones. The woods get lusher, the trees larger, the greens more variegated and vibrant.

A few hours after we make camp in the primeval woods, Dave catches up.

"What do you guys think?" he asks. His ear-to-ear grin leaves no doubt at all what kind of day he's had. "Does it get any better than this?"

I've had many great days in other great places, all of them unique. But a better day is beyond my experience, beyond my imagination. I don't think it can exist. Today makes up for all the bad days behind us, and quite possibly for any to come.

September 29. Day 147. Mile 2,517. Sitcum Creek.

It's 6:30. I've made a liter of herbal tea and am sitting by the fire. Despite the dry day, the lower forests are still soaking wet, so we started the fire with dry wood we tore from the insides of a rotting tree stump.

Earlier today we said goodbye to Squirrel and Knees, and Kirk and Conrad. And just now, we said goodbye to Dave, too, although we only met him a couple of days ago. Special K is already ahead; he's pressed for time and left a day early from Skykomish. The rest of them are planning to get to Stehekin (and therefore Canada) one day ahead of us. Wanchor is apparently a day behind. He left Skykomish with everyone else, but bailed out when it started to rain. I hope the weather holds because I can't help but think how dangerous and exposed the above-treeline traverse we just did would be in bad weather. Already a fresh batch of dark clouds are moving in. Only 10 days until the end. I'll use the memories of today to stay positive and focused in the days to come.

—DAN'S JOURNAL

That's all, folks. One good day.

In the morning, we break camp under threatening skies. By eleven o'clock it's raining again. And yet again, I've readjusted my definition of good weather. This time, the clouds are high in the sky, hovering right about at Glacier Peak's 10,544-foot summit. So we can see the mountain. Just now, I don't care if it's raining as long as I can see the mountain.

Glacier Peak is dramatic and powerful, and I find myself stopping every hundred yards or so simply to stare at its ravished glaciated facade. Built up on a pre-existing ridge, it is the most glacially eroded volcanic peak in the North Cascades. Its last eruption, 12,000 years ago, was second only to the eruption of Mazama that created Crater Lake. Glacier Peak won't permit a trail high on its flanks; there are too many glaciers, too many avalanche slopes. So the trail cowers down lower. But that doesn't make the walking easy.

This is a mountain gouged from base to summit by its glacial streams. On the lower slopes, the drainages have etched deep valleys between intervening ridges. Our route is thus a matter of climbing over one of these side ridges, plummeting into a valley, climbing back over another ridge, and so on.

View of Tower Mountain from Granite Pass, Mount Baker National Forest

Above Grasshopper Pass, Mount Baker National Forest

It seems that we spend days climbing around Glacier Peak. We keep thinking we must be finished with it, only to top another ridge and see its gray-white facade still glowering at us. Three thousand feet up; three thousand feet down; and so on and so forth, through fog and rain and mist. Above treeline, the winds are fierce.

In this vertical landscape, there are only two places to camp: either at the bottom of a valley or at the top of a ridge, rarely anywhere in between. We end up doing much longer days than we had planned because it just seems to make more sense to keep walking than to huddle in a soaking wet campsite.

But the walking itself is beautiful, as lovely as any sunny ridgeline traverse. We now are spending most of our time down in the old growth forests. These are the legendary forests of the Pacific Northwest, with western redcedars that can be 10, 12, or even more feet in diameter, along with Douglas firs, silver firs, and western hemlocks. A man we met in Skykomish told us about finding a western redcedar that was 42 feet in circumference.

And the best way to see this forest is in rain.

Just now, walking in the rain has become something magical. Because these forests are formed by rain; they belong in the rain. Seeing them in the rain focuses your attention up close, where it needs to be. A thousand shades of green catch your eye. The soft, rain-filtered light illuminates a million subtleties: the Wolf's lichen that drips from trunks and branches like the green beard of a forest elf, the neon mosses, the mushrooms (purple ones, yellow ones, orange, red, white, beige, brown—even blue and green) that push their way out of the earth like miniature bulldozers, fully grown, able to lift a whole pound of dirt and shove it aside; the nurse logs—fallen trees that support and feed a whole community of baby plants—covered in moss and spouting ferns and seedlings, all of them decorated with raindrop ornaments. Crystal clear streams pool on gravel shelves, looking as pure as water could ever be. The smell of the forest is clean and fecund at the same time.

It is a place as dramatic and beautiful as the panorama from any alpine pass.

Like the Alpine Lakes Wilderness, this area was controversial when first proposed as wilderness. The reason is simple: money. I once interviewed a Forest Service timber manager about the value of old-growth forests. I was trying to learn the value of timber that couldn't be sold in order to enable a single pair of endangered Oregon spotted owls to live and breed. The figures I got were 3,000 acres (that's the estimated territory for a breeding pair of spotted owls), and a total of $144 million "on the stump" (that is, the approximate amount a timber company would pay the Forest Service to log that 3,000 acres). Logging advocates like to use figures like this to prove how ridiculously expensive it is to save the spotted owl. How can a spotted owl be worth $144 million, they ask, inviting you to agree that it can't. But it seems to me that this has nothing to do with owls: selling our old-growth forests at $48,000 an acre is a crime. It's like bulldozing the Louvre to steal its building materials.

DAN EATING LUNCH AT RED PASS

October 2. Day 150. Mile 2,551. Trailside camp near Canyon 4.980.

Neither Karen nor I wanted to voice the possibility that we could actually make it into Stehekin tomorrow, a day early. We didn't want to get our hopes up. But the weather pushed us ahead of schedule, and by the time we reached Suiattle Pass this afternoon, we realized that we might make it. The trick is reaching the trailhead before the last shuttle bus leaves for town.

We are camped just past a huge canyon on the side of a ridge between Plummer and Sitting Bull mountains. The canyon was cluttered with boulders the size of trucks and houses. I felt like a Lilliputian, making my way among them. In the mist and fog, we couldn't find the campsite described in the guidebook, so we walked on until dark, when we threw our stuff down on the only flat spot we could find, which happened to be the trail. It's not like we'll be in anyone's way tonight.

—DAN'S JOURNAL

Stehekin is not a place you can get to by car. You can arrive by boat, seaplane, or foot; cars have to be ferried in. Once they arrive, they can drive up and down a two-way dead-end road.

Hence there is a Park Service shuttle to take hikers to and from the trailheads. This time of year, it runs only twice a day. Our goal is to be there by 3:30 in the afternoon, and despite muddy trail, blisters, and a couple of instances where we aren't sure exactly where the trail goes, we arrive there early.

Now the challenge is to stay warm until the shuttle leaves. Before the driver can take us into town, he has to drive up to another trailhead to see if any poor souls are shivering up there, waiting for a ride.

The town is as offbeat as you'd expect of a place you can't drive to. The store, which is also the lodge office, is the most sparsely supplied on the entire Pacific Crest Trail, an honor for which it overcame tough competition. Locals get groceries by faxing orders to a supermarket in Chelan, which fills the orders and ships them out via the ferry. For tourists, there's a lodge, a restaurant, and a small outfitter. A post office, a bakery, and a laundry room serve both locals and hikers.

We are now officially obsessed with getting dry and staying that way. The day is consumed with chores. Kirk and Conrad (to no-one's surprise, we've all regrouped again) are spraying waterproofing compound on their tent. Knees is experimenting with trying to get the oven in the cabin to stay at about 100 degrees in order to dry out boots. Dan has bought supplies (extra fuel for our stove, energy bars because they don't get soggy when you eat them in the rain) and is rubbing wax into our boots, which I have declined to put in the oven. Dave is making phone calls trying to find out a weather forecast. I'm doing laundry, and while I'm waiting for the machines, I'm also studying maps of the trails trying to figure out alternate routes and bailout points in case we get weather we shouldn't be stuck out in.

"Joe says we should make a run for the border."

Joe is Joe Sobinovsky at the Pacific Crest Trail Association, who has been fielding phones calls from thru-hikers for the last half a year.

"The snow-line is dropping," Dave tells us. "Joe says the storms are lined up one after the other, and there's no break in sight. He thinks this is the end of the season. But he thinks we can make it."

The last big push.

It's a 3,000-foot climb from the Stehekin road to Rainy Pass, but the climb keeps us warm despite the cold rain.

Rainy Pass gives us no reason to question its name. We stop for lunch under the shelter of a latrine on the north side of the pass. It's early in the afternoon, and we're trying to figure out whether it makes sense to go on. The guidebook doesn't give us much information about likely campsites up ahead; the map shows a trail that is going to be traversing steep slopes and climbing 3,000 feet in the next 5 miles. And what is rain down here is snow on the pass. It makes more sense to stay low and sheltered. But a cryptic remark in the guidebook about lavish restroom facilities at the parking lot on the south side of the pass makes us wonder whether they might offer better shelter than our pit toilet.

So we retreat to the other side, where the new, spacious restroom facility is closed for the season. But a large roof hanging over the entrance gives enough shelter for at least two tents, maybe three. We don't even stop to think: immediately, we pitch our tent on the concrete floor under the roof. Periodically, people drive up to the parking lot and walk over to see if the restrooms are open. They look at us in the defensive way you look at someone you think might hurt you. After all, what normal person pitches a tent under the roof of a bathroom?

We helpfully explain that the bathrooms are locked, but that there is a latrine behind the building that is open. Nobody has the nerve to ask what we're doing here.

All in all, we're grateful for the accommodations.

The next morning dawns predictably wet and gray. At first it seems no different than any other morning. But as we climb out of the pass, the rain quickly turns to fat wet snowflakes. At first, they are pretty on the trees and no trouble underfoot. Up we go.

View of sunset from Slate Peak, Mount Baker National Forest

Harts Pass area, Mount Baker National Forest

Benson Basin and Mount Ballard, Pasayten Wilderness

Distant Mount Ballard, Pasayten Wilderness

As we climb, the trees get thinner and the snow gets deeper: it seems to be gaining about an inch in depth for every 100 feet we climb. By the time we've climbed 1,000 feet, I poke my trekking-pole into the snow and measure 10 inches of accumulation. We still have nearly 2,000 feet to go.

Even this low down, the snow has virtually obscured the trail. We can still find it, because the trail is a swath through vegetation. But what about up higher, where there are no trees, less vegetation, and the slopes are open? How will we be able to find a trail under snow when there is almost no visibility in the swirling snow and wind? The long-term forecast is for more of the same followed by more of the same.

I'm breaking trail. It's a lot more work to break trail than to follow someone. I'm in the lead, and I don't want to ask Dan to take over because I know what's going to happen if we stop to talk about this. It is not sensible to be continuing up. If I don't talk about the snow, I won't have to admit that this is a pretty stupid thing to be doing.

But after an hour and a half, I'm getting tired. I turn to Dan and say, "Would you mind breaking trail for a while?"

"Sure," he says.

It's the first conversation we've had since the snow started falling.

I step aside and he passes me, not saying anything.

"Good," I think.

"What do you think about this?" he asks in a neutral tone of voice.

One innocent little question.

"I was really hoping you wouldn't ask," I say.

Because now we have to admit that we both know enough to know that we need to turn around. We still have almost 2,000 feet to climb. Given the accumulation down here and the rate at which it is increasing, the snow up on the ridge is probably more than 2 feet deep, possibly much more. Slogging through that would be slow going if we could even see where we were going, which we are not going to be able to do. Navigating through 65 miles in these conditions is something we know better than to attempt, especially wearing boots and socks that are soaking wet from yesterday's rain. And this is wilderness—real wilderness. Once we're in it, bailing out will be as much of an adventure as going through.

There is no need to have a discussion. Dan and I both know better. We just didn't want to.

We turn around and head back down.

Since we were the first ones up, we're the ones who get to break the news to the others. I relate the conditions as objectively as I can. The younger guys are stronger than I am, so I'm hesitant to tell them what they can or can't do. In my long-distance hiking career, I've seen a lot of people do a lot of remarkable things. But I honestly can't imagine how tough you'd have to be to walk 65 miles, mostly above treeline, in a North Cascades winter whiteout. We pass on the news, and the guys decide to bail out with us—not, however, before checking it out for themselves.

So what now?

We hitchhike to Mazama, the nearest town, which is about 30 miles away, and for once luck is with us: a mini-van stops and we manage to pile all seven of us in, including packs. I'm in awe of the driver and his wife for being brave enough to stop for a crew that defines the word motley.

Mazama is in the rain shadow, on the eastern side of the Cascades. It is sunny, sort of.

Now the decision-making begins.

We can wait down here for the weather to clear, if and when it does. But the forecast is for more storms; they're lined up like balls in a pitching machine.

We can just stop right here, declare victory, pop open the Champagne and start the celebration now. That's one option Kirk and Conrad are considering, although they keep changing their minds. The way

KAREN AT THE BORDER MONUMENT

they see it, they've done the PCT. Not hiking the last 65 miles isn't going to lessen their sense of accomplishment, or ruin their memories of a terrific six-month adventure. It's not like there's a brass band waiting for any of us at the border. They do, however, want to get to Manning Park, because their families have treated them to a celebratory night in the lodge.

Another choice is to continue to walk to Canada, but not on the actual PCT. We can cobble together a route from roads and other trails. The problem is, information is hard to find, especially about where those trails and roads end up once they cross into Canada. Kirk and Conrad are considering walking a road on the eastern side of the mountains, low down and out of the rain. Dan and I are definitely walking to Canada, but I refuse to walk on a paved road for 65 miles just to say I did it, so we're looking at a trail that runs along Ross Lake, just a few miles west of the official PCT. For Squirrel and Knees, the most important thing is to "connect the footsteps," in order to have an unbroken walk from Mexico to Canada. They're also trying to find a way to reconnect with the PCT so they can cross into Canada at the trail's official terminus. The problem is, all of the trails that reconnect to the PCT cross passes that are exposed and above 6,000 feet.

One way or the other, we have to decide. The weather forecasts predict that the snow level could be down below 2,000 feet in the next couple of days—meaning that even the lower Ross Lake route could be snow-covered if we wait too much longer.

Every once in a while, someone wonders if we couldn't just bite the bullet, do 30 miles a day, and be done with it. But that's wishful thinking. The high snow accumulations, the lack of visibility, the projected forecast, and our lack of winter expedition gear, mean that the PCT is off-limits, too risky to contemplate. Sometimes, the mountains just say no.

In the end it's Ross Lake for all of us. The walk is uneventful, pretty, easy, and fast. At this lower elevation, autumn colors are almost New England-like, with bright yellow vine maples covering the forest floor. We keep looking up at the mountains wondering if we could have made it, but not second-guessing our decision. It's only a two-and-a-half-day walk. The last full day starts out drizzly, but then a rainbow slices across the lake and the sun comes out. Dan and I camp that night at one of the prettiest sites of the trip, overlooking a lake shadowed by snowy peaks. Up there somewhere, where the mountains are white, is the trail.

The rest of the group goes blasting past us, bringing yet another foul weather report, this one from a ranger. Rain and snow tomorrow, a big storm. "Well, what else is new?" Dan and I say.

What's new is the next morning we beat the storm to the border.

As we're walking up the road to Monument 72, we meet Squirrel and Knees and Dave coming back to take a ferry across the lake to a lodge from which they'll make their way to Seattle and home. Kirk and Conrad have gotten a ride out and are headed for the lodge in Manning Park. And we're waiting for Bart Smith, whose photographic journey inspired this book, to meet us and photograph the last minutes of our pilgrimage.

At the border monument, the other hikers have left a Ziploc bag with a note under a rock, copying the tradition of leaving a note in Monument 78, which marks the PCT's entrance into Canada. Their note declared this to be the "official alternate end of the Pacific Crest Trail." We add our names to theirs, reflecting how appropriate this is, after all.

From beginning to end, this trail has challenged, delighted, dismayed, frustrated, entertained, taught, and surprised us. That here we are on the Canadian border, on the wrong trail, at the wrong monument is, I think, emblematic of the whole experience.

On the PCT, anything can happen.

And it did.

On the slopes of Tamarack Peak, Pasayten Wilderness

View of North Cascades from Lakeview Ridge, Pasayten Wilderness

AFTERWORD

We no longer worry about keeping the toilet paper dry. Or matches, or our down sleeping bags, or our warm clothes or extra socks. We no longer ask strangers if they know the latest weather forecast, or look for mares' tails in the sky and coronas around the moon. We no longer measure our hours by footsteps, our days by miles.

Instead, we have been reintroduced to the television, and rush-hour traffic, and the telephone, and deadlines. Especially deadlines.

A thru-hiker returning home can feel a lot like a deer caught in the headlights of a speeding truck. Things that used to seem ordinary have become anything but. Even driving a car is no longer automatic. After five months of traveling at the pace of two or three miles an hour, our first foray in an automobile—driving along Interstate 5 in Seattle during rush hour—felt like a ride in amusement park bumper cars. We cowered in the right lane at 40 miles per hour and wondered where everyone was going to in such a hurry, and why they needed to run us over to get there. (This is not an experience we would recommend to future PCT hikers.)

Or lights. In the woods, the full moon seemed shockingly bright, more than bright enough to light the night. Now our nights are lit by street lights and office buildings and a zillion cars.

Fitness is no longer just a routine part of our everyday lives. We have to schedule time for exercise, feel guilty if we miss a day, worry about how we're going to squeeze in a run when we've got 12-hour work days and there's 8 inches of snow on the ground.

And then there is *stuff*. For five months, we clothed and fed and sheltered ourselves with what was in our backpacks. We always had what we needed. We were never bored. Now we have stuff: computers, books, clothes, CDs, kitchen stuff, bathroom stuff. Stuff to pack, stuff to unpack, stuff to put away, to organize, to worry about.

LUPINE AND INDIAN PAINTBRUSH, ALPINE LAKES WILDERNESS

As we slowly but surely trade the rhythms of the walking life for the routines of the so-called real world, it's worth remembering what our old friend John Muir has to say:

The mountains are fountains not only of rivers and fertile soil, but of men. Therefore we are all, in some sense mountaineers, and going into the mountains is going home. Yet how many are doomed to toil in towns' shadows while the white mountains beckon all along the horizon.

The mountains are still beckoning. It turns out that we are not yet finished with the PCT, or it with us. When we left the trail in October, we had already decided to return to Washington in order to see the state in good weather. (Bart's pictures convinced us that Washington occasionally has good weather.) So as this book is hitting the stores, we are once again on the trail.

A few months after finishing our thru-hike, we started receiving holiday cards from trail friends. We're all slowly readjusting to life in the civilized lane, going back to work, organizing our stuff. Some of our fellow hikers are already dreaming about the next big trip.

We would suggest that while a thru-hike is certainly not for everybody, neither is toiling in the shadows of towns. A walk in the woods can be the antidote to what ails most of us, if we just make the time—if only for a day or a weekend. Our system of national scenic trails boasts some of the finest walking in the world. The benefits include fitness, self-reliance, and the experience of living only and completely in the present moment—an experience that is fast being stolen by the ever-increasing pressures of what passes for civilization.

The mountains are beckoning. Answer the call.

—KAREN BERGER AND DANIEL R. SMITH

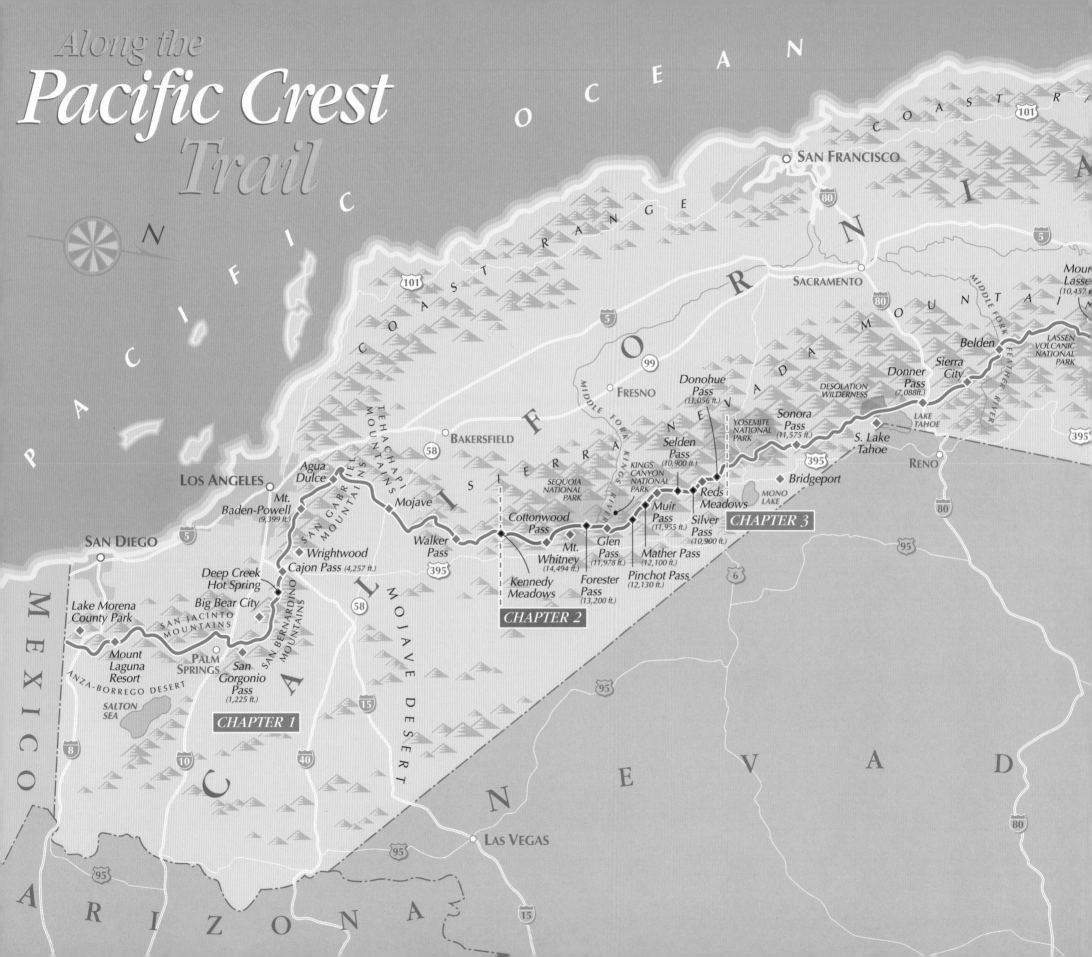

Along the
Pacific Crest
Trail

PACIFIC OCEAN

COAST RANGE

SIERRA NEVADA MOUNTAINS

MIDDLE FORK FEATHER RIVER

MIDDLE FORK KINGS RIVER

SAN FRANCISCO

SACRAMENTO

Mount Lassen (10,457 ft.)

LASSEN VOLCANIC NATIONAL PARK

Belden

Sierra City

Donner Pass (7,088 ft.)

DESOLATION WILDERNESS

LAKE TAHOE

S. Lake Tahoe

Reno

Sonora Pass (11,575 ft.)

Donohue Pass (11,056 ft.)

Selden Pass (10,900 ft.)

YOSEMITE NATIONAL PARK

Bridgeport

MONO LAKE

CHAPTER 3

FRESNO

KINGS CANYON NATIONAL PARK

Muir Pass (11,955 ft.)

Silver Pass (10,900 ft.)

Reds Meadows

Mather Pass (12,100 ft.)

Pinchot Pass (12,130 ft.)

SEQUOIA NATIONAL PARK

BAKERSFIELD

Agua Dulce

TEHACHAPI MOUNTAINS

Mojave

SAN GABRIEL MOUNTAINS

Mt. Baden-Powell (9,399 ft.)

LOS ANGELES

Walker Pass

Cottonwood Pass

Mt. Whitney (14,494 ft.)

Glen Pass (11,978 ft.)

Forester Pass (13,200 ft.)

Kennedy Meadows

CHAPTER 2

Wrightwood

Cajon Pass (4,257 ft.)

SAN BERNARDINO MOUNTAINS

Deep Creek Hot Spring

Big Bear City

SAN JACINTO MOUNTAINS

SAN DIEGO

Lake Morena County Park

Mount Laguna Resort

ANZA-BORREGO DESERT

SALTON SEA

PALM SPRINGS

San Gorgonio Pass (1,225 ft.)

MOJAVE DESERT

CHAPTER 1

MEXICO

ARIZONA

NEVADA

LAS VEGAS

CALIFORNIA